The Harvard Institute For International Development And Its Antecedents

Edward S. Mason

Monographs on Development

Published by

Harvard Institute for International
Harvard University

and

University Press of America

University Press of America,® Inc.

4720 Boston Way
Lanham, MD 20706

3 Henrietta Street
London WC2E 8LU England

Printed in the United States of America

Co-published by arrangement with the
Harvard Institute for International Development

Library of Congress Cataloging in Publication Data

Mason, Edward Sagendorph, 1899-
The Harvard Institute for International Development
and its antecedents.

Bibliography: p.
1. Harvard Institute for International Development.
2. Economic development projects—Developing countries.
3. Developing countries—Economic conditions.
I. Harvard Institute for International Development.
II. Title.
HC59.72.E44M37 1986 338.9'006'07444 86-13240
ISBN 0-8191-5552-7 (alk. paper)
ISBN 0-8191-5553-5 (pbk. : alk. paper)

All University Press of America books are produced on acid-free
paper which exceeds the minimum standards set by the National
Historical Publications and Records Commission.

Contents

Foreword

Given today's widespread concern with development it is difficult to recall that a scant thirty years ago relatively little analytic work had been done on the conditions that characterize Third World countries and that few universities offered courses dealing with development or encouraged their faculty to work in developing countries. Yet some of the economists who had played significant roles in shaping American national and international policies during the war years were impressed with the importance of the underdeveloped countries for the future of the United States and of world peace. Edward S. Mason was one of those who both saw the needs of the developing countries and recognized the importance of formulating policies that would accelerate their economic growth and improve the welfare of their populations.

In 1954–55, Edward Mason, then Dean of the Graduate School of Public Administration, Harvard University directed an eight–person team which drew up a plan for the economic development of Pakistan and in 1958 he organized a similar effort for the Government of Iran. These initial efforts to involve University staff in the development process eventually led to the formation of the Development Advisory Service and subsequently to the establishment of the Harvard Institute for International Development. Although as Ed says in his own preface he was less directly involved in the transition in 1974 from the DAS to the Harvard Institute for International Development, the research, teaching and advisory activities of HIID are still largely shaped by his earlier vision. Ed also recognized the pressing need to train the staffs of various economic ministries in the Third World and in 1957 a training program for mid–career officials from developing countries was started at Harvard University. This program, now called the Edward S. Mason Program, in honor of its founder, has over five hundred and fifty alumni from nearly sixty countries and continues to be administered by the Institute.

The DAS was founded twenty–four years ago and the earlier advisory efforts go back roughly thirty years. Aspects of this long period of work have been covered by other studies but no one has written a comprehensive overview of how HIID evolved. Some of the information necessary for such a study is written down in annual reports and other documents, but much of it resides in the memories of those who participated. It was for this reason that HIID asked Ed Mason if he would undertake to write up his own perspective on how this Institute came to be. The essay contained herein is the result of that effort. It is first of all Ed Mason's personal view of how the Institute evolved and it emphasizes the early period when he was most actively involved in giving it leadership and direction. But the essay also draws on documents in the Institute files and on the recollections of others who participated in the process, so that it is much more than a collection of personal memories.

Someday a scholar or scholars may see fit to write a full–blown "official" history of the DAS–HIID. When that time comes, this essay will be that effort's most valuable primary source.

Cambridge, MA
January 1986

Dwight H. Perkins, Director
Harvard Institute for
International Development

Preface

This account of the Harvard Institute for International Development (HIID) and its antecedents inevitably reflects my changing relations to the events under discussion. The projects in Pakistan and Iran were directly under my supervision and are here discussed at what some may feel to be disproportionate lengths. During the period of the Development Advisory Service (DAS), 1962 to 1974, I was, until my retirement in 1969, chairman of the advisory committee and, during this whole period, a close observer of Cambridge and overseas activities. In the HIID period, 1974 to date, I have been merely an onlooker, though an interested and curious one.

The result has been an admittedly uneven treatment of the subject. With respect to Pakistan and Iran and the various projects undertaken under DAS auspices, I have felt myself competent to undertake an assessment of performance. I have not attempted to do this for the various projects undertaken by HIID. Here I have limited myself to describing changes in the relationship of the institution to the University, to changes in the character of the overseas projects undertaken and their financing, and to an account of the teaching and research activities of HIID. I leave it to others more familiar with recent activities to evaluate results.

It should not have been necessary for my attention to have been called to the great contribution the wives of advisors have made to the success of Harvard's overseas projects, but I confess it was. Not only did they help their husbands survive in often difficult environments but almost invariably they made a direct contribution by organizing schools, serving in hospitals, and participating in a variety of local activities. The success of overseas projects was heavily dependent on them. I hope I may be forgiven for not emphasizing their contribution.

This manuscript has been read by David C. Cole, Lester E. Gordon, Richard D. Mallon, Dwight H. Perkins, Donald R. Snodgrass, Joseph J. Stern, and Francis X. Sutton, and has been greatly improved by their comments. I am responsible for any errors of fact or interpretation which remain.

Cambridge, 1985 E.S.M.

Introduction

The Harvard Institute for International Development is the present name of an organization which, together with its antecedents, has undertaken a series of overseas projects concerned with the economic development of less developed countries (LDCs), with research on the development process, with teaching, and with the assembly of teaching materials for use in Harvard courses on economic and political development. The history of HIID falls into three parts. The first stage saw the undertaking of advisory projects to the planning organizations of Pakistan (1954) and Iran (1958) administered by the Graduate School of Public Administration. The second stage was the formation in 1962 of the Development Advisory Service, which conducted a series of overseas projects under the aegis of the Center for International Affairs. The present stage began in 1974 with the formation of HIID, which attempted both to broaden the scope areas of assistance to LDCs and to increase the participation of various schools and departments of the University in overseas activities. Currently HIID is an independent organization within the University whose director reports to the Dean of the Faculty of Arts and Sciences, who in turn chairs a committee of six deans. Finally, HIID is advised by a faculty council made up of members of schools and departments interested in its activities.

Although HIID is not the only Harvard institution administering projects in the less developed world—the School of Public Health, the Graduate School of Education, the Graduate School of Design, the Law School, and the Business School have all been active at one time or another—it is the largest and most developed. And, although still predominantly staffed by economists, it has sought to involve in recent activities representatives from other schools of the University.

The history of HIID also includes an ancillary activity, the training of government officials from less developed countries. The training program started in 1957 with seven government officials from India, Pakistan, Burma, and Indonesia. In recent years, about fifty per year (representing, over time, practically all the countries of Asia, Africa, and Latin America) have been registered in the John F. Kennedy School of Government. The relationship of this training program to HIID remains close. Many of these officials come from countries in which HIID has had or has projects; their teaching is to a considerable extent undertaken by HIID staff, and teaching materials heavily emphasize HIID's overseas experience. They are also effective spokesmen, when they return to their own countries, concerning HIID's expertise.

These Harvard overseas activities and the training program for government officials have now been in operation for a little more than twenty-five years and there have been substantial changes. The first two projects consisted of advisory services to planning commissions. There is little demand for such services now. Many LDCs feel fully competent to staff their own commissions and dispense with foreign advice. Furthermore, this is an area which most countries regard as highly sensitive. The work of HIID overseas advisors has tended to become more technical and specialized. Agricultural development, trade and fiscal policies, assistance in the formation of research organizations, and training programs are now more frequent areas of overseas activities and, increasingly, advice on management, health services, and education is sought. These changes in the focus of overseas activities are reflected in the HIID research and in the teaching of economic and political development at Harvard.

Although the financing of HIID activities and related training programs now comes from many sources, in the early years the Ford Foundation was predominant. The Foundation financed the advisory missions in Pakistan and Iran; it provided a necessary reserve for the Development Advisory Service; it covered all the expenses of the first few classes of government officials brought to Harvard for training; and it contributed substantially to later DAS and HIID projects. In the 1950s and '60s, the Ford Foundation maintained representatives in all the Asian and South American countries in which the DAS was involved—Iran, Pakistan, Indonesia, Malaysia, Argentina, and Colombia—and the Ford offices provided administrative services to DAS activities. They found houses and furnishings for overseas advisors, helped clear goods through customs, and performed other tasks that required knowledge of local practices. It is not too much to say that the Ford Foundation financed the framework of the activities later taken over by HIID.

1. The First Stage: The Harvard Advisory Groups

Pakistan: The Early Years

In 1953, as Dean of the Graduate School of Public Administration, I was visited by Randall Klemme, Ford Foundation representative in Pakistan, to seek my help in organizing a group to advise the newly founded Planning Board in that country. India's First Five–Year Plan was in progress and the event created great interest. Pakistan felt it must also have a five–year plan. David Bell, former advisor to President Truman, later to be Budget Director and head of the Agency for International Development, was in Cambridge that year and was at somewhat loose ends. I persuaded him that this venture might be of some interest, and in October 1953 we spent two weeks in Pakistan interviewing the newly appointed head of the Planning Board, Zahid Husain, and the Minister of Finance, Chaudri Muhamad Ali, the man to whom the Planning Board reported.

I attempted mildly to suggest to these officials that perhaps of more use than a Five–Year Plan would be a small staff of technicians working with local counterparts on matters of current economic policy, but neither was receptive to this suggestion. In the end it was agreed that Bell and I would return to Cambridge and recruit eight advisors of specified qualifications. At that time the Planning Board consisted of its Chairman, and a deputy secretary, Mushtaq Ilahi. But, by the time the advisors began to arrive in Karachi in the spring of 1954, eight or ten Pakistanis had been selected to work with the advisors. The contract, involving Harvard, the Government of Pakistan, and the Ford Foundation, was to run for 18 months beginning March 1, 1954. The shortness of the contract reflected misgivings on the part of all three contractors concerning the effectiveness of this venture. David Bell was the resident director of the project and Gustav Papanek his deputy. The eight advisors included six Americans and two Canadians.

The period to be covered by the First Five–year Plan was 1955 to 1960, and it was obvious that a barely organized Planning Board could not be expected to present a plan to the government before the beginning of the Plan period. In any event, a draft plan was not available until June 1956. After discussions with ministries of the central government and the governments of Pakistan's two provinces, the revised plan was accepted in the spring of 1958. The planning period was by then halfway finished, and it would be difficult to find any resemblance between what was recommended in the Plan and what in fact got done. This does not mean, however, that the Plan was a useless exercise. Its chief accomplishment was to serve as an intellectual framework for the organization of data relating to central issues of development.

This first plan was, for its day, an unusual document in emphasizing certain priorities neglected in most contemporary plans. The first Pakistan Plan (in sharp contrast to the first Indian Plan and many others) gave top priority to agriculture and rural development rather than industry. It also placed great emphasis (in a chapter personally written by Zahid Husain) on the need for improving public management. And the first Plan (at the urging of Husain not the Harvard advisors) recommended prompt attention to the rapid growth of population. Not a bad record for 1956.

The first contract was scheduled to end September 1, 1955. The Chairman of the Planning Board and the Minister of Finance asked for a two year renewal but there was opposition in some quarters. The Secretary of the Ministry of Economic Affairs would have preferred that the contract not be extended because the Harvard advisors were not sufficiently under his control—they insisted on reporting solely to the Chairman of the Planning Board. And the representative of the Ford Foundation in Pakistan did not want the contract extended unless the Harvard advisors gave their advice through him, a model he believed he saw, and envied, in the Ford Foundation representative in India. Matters were briefly at a standstill until the Ford Foundation replaced their representative with George Gant, who had been an educational advisor in Pakistan, and the objections of the Secretary were overcome.

The second contract ended September 1, 1957. By that time there had been a number of changes both on the Planning Board and in the advisory group. The Board had become a Commission and the Prime Minister had become chairman with the operating head as vice-chairman. The Pakistani staff had increased to 20–25 and planning units had been established in the provinces. The advisory group had increased to fourteen with ten in Karachi and two each in Lahore and Dacca. A number of consultants had paid short visits to Pakistan including Wassily Leontief and Hollis Chenery from Harvard. As the Dean reported,

> Although we have accomplished what the program originally intended, i.e., to give assistance to the Government of Pakistan in the preparation of its development program, both the Government and the Ford Foundation have pressed the view that much remains to be done before this type of staff operation can be said to be firmly established in the Central Government and in the two Provincial Governments. Consequently, I have agreed to renew the contract for a three–year period on condition that our cooperation then comes to an end.[1]

This turned out to be wishful thinking. After several more renewals, each urged strongly by planning officials, and with different financing, the project ended in 1970. On the basis of hindsight I would have to say that this was about five years too long. It would have been better to have ended the connection in 1965 when both the Planning Commission and the Harvard Advisory Group had reached a high point of their effectiveness. But, on this, more later.

At the end of the first contract five of the advisors returned home leaving Bell and Papanek to recruit, with assistance from Cambridge, a second and enlarged group. Among the second wave were a number of distinguished economists including Clair Wilcox of Swarthmore and Emile Despres, chairman of the economics department at Williams. Despres, in particular, made a large contribution, not only to the work of the Planning Board (later Commission), but also to research and training. He later organized a training program for government officials at Williams College, modeled after the Harvard Public Service Program. He also helped establish the Pakistan Institute of Development Economics, which brought a number of able foreign economists to Karachi to work on development research with a group of Pakistani counterparts. This organization published the *Pakistan Development Review*, which for many years, was one of the most—if not the most—distinguished economics journals in the underdeveloped world.[2]

Work on the Second Five–Year Development Program began as soon as the government had accepted the first. This was a decidedly more professional job and it was accepted by the government before the beginning of the second plan period, 1960–1965. Bell and Papanek returned to Cambridge in 1958 to assist in managing the project and in teaching courses in development economics. Harry Case, director of personnel in the Tennessee Valley Authority, became project supervisor and he and his team worked with the new head of the Planning Commission, G. Ahmed.

I shall return to a discussion and evaluation of the work of the Pakistan project presently. One observation relating to its first six years, which is borne out by experience elsewhere, needs to be emphasized. Economic development requires a government capable of governing and one that assigns a high priority to economic development. This, during the period in question, Pakistan did not have. Four prime ministers heading four different governments took turns in Karachi. The highest priority of all these governments was the maintenance of law and order, a problem exacerbated by the forced immigration of 6.5 million Muslims from India. Scarcely a year went by in the 1950s that did not see large-scale rioting in some large city. As a qualified observer remarked in 1959, "There have been few months since 1947 when some larger center was not 'under section 144' [that section of the Criminal Code permitting a magistrate to bar all public gatherings]."[3] Under these circumstances the maintenance of law and order became a chief, if not *the* chief, preoccupation of both the central and the provincial governments. And economic development suffered.

Iran

A second overseas project undertaken under the auspices of the School of Public Administration involved Iran.[4] In 1957, I was visited by Mr. Abolhassan Ebtehaj, the managing director of the Plan Organization of Iran. Ebtehaj had sought advice from the World Bank on whether the Plan Organization should establish an economic advisory unit, and a member of the bank staff, John Adler, had prepared a report for him on the use of economists in planning operations. The Adler Report had recommended the establishment of such a unit to assist in the completion of the Second Plan and to help prepare a Third Plan. Ebtehaj was a forceful, impressive fellow and the Plan Organization an unusual government agency. Earlier, Ebtehaj had been president of the Bank Melli, the central bank of Iran, and in that capacity had established a unit in the Bank concerned with development planning. He had also persuaded government authorities to employ two overseas consulting firms, Morrison-Knudsen and Overseas Consultants, Inc., to prepare a list of projects deemed to have high priority for Iranian development. Selections from this list constituted the work program for the First Seven-Year Plan and for much of the Second.

The first Plan Law was enacted in 1949 and the Plan was intended to cover the period 1949 to 1956. This intention was frustrated, however, by the oil crisis which brought Mossadegh to power and led to the Shah's temporary absence from the country. When Mossadegh's rule had been undermined, with an undercover but real assist from the United States, and the Shah had returned in 1953, it was decided to scrap the remainder of the First Plan and proceed to the Second. The project list prepared by the overseas consultants still embraced the "candidate projects" from which the Plan Organization was expected to develop and finance the highest priority investments. The Plan Organization was not a planning commission in the ordinary sense of the term but more in the nature of a development corporation or public works ministry. When regular government ministries were deemed capable of undertaking a project, the Plan Organization acted as financier and supervisor. When this was judged by the Plan Organization not to be the case, the Organization itself became the administrator.

Ebtehaj became Managing Director at the beginning of the Second Seven–Year Plan in 1954 and, with strong support from the Shah, gave a forceful administration to the Plan Organization. He was one of the few men in Iran who dared say "no" to the Shah. Apparently he said "no" once too often and was peremptorily removed from office in August of 1959. The last time I saw him he was a prisoner, albeit a well–treated one, in a military hospital. In Iran, favored positions could be rapidly lost but also rapidly regained. During the next few years Ebtehaj became the principal owner and manager of a respected private bank. He is now in retirement in France.

The Plan Organization, as it was in 1958 when the Harvard Advisory Group began an assignment that was to last for four years, received most of its financing from a share of Iran's oil revenues which were then running at $300 to $400 million a year. But Plan Organization projects were also financed by the World Bank, the U.S. Agency for International Development, and other sources. The Plan Organization had to battle continuously for its share of oil revenues with the regular ministries of government and this natural antagonism of interests was exacerbated by Ebtehaj's frequently well–justified reluctance to trust ministries to administer Plan Organization funds for the construction and management of development projects. Increasingly the Plan Organization was known as a government within a government. This situation could last as long as the Plan Organization acted primarily as a development corporation and as long as Ebtehaj enjoyed the strong support of the Shah.

But, when the Plan Organization began to venture into comprehensive planning, relations with various ministries became critical and the fall from grace of Ebtehaj little short of catastrophic. This was the situation the Harvard Group confronted in Iran not long after its arrival.

Ebtehaj was not only a strong but also an imaginative administrator. Not content to rely on a list of projects prepared some years before by the overseas consultants, he authorized surveys and investigations designed to explore the problems of various sectors of the economy and to elucidate development priorities. For this purpose the existing staff of the Plan Organization was not well suited. In private conversation at the time of his appointment, Ebtehaj described the Plan Organization as "demoralized" and "incapable of doing effective planning without assistance from foreign experts." As a result of his request to the World Bank, a professional engineering advisory service known as the Technical Bureau was established in 1955. A consulting firm from the United States, the Government Affairs Institute, was engaged to work on the Agency's administrative problems. The economic advisory group from Harvard added to Plan Organization's already sizable foreign contingent. And because of the character of many of the projects (large dams, irrigation works, and road systems), which were beyond the competence of Iranian contractors, foreign construction and management firms were brought in to manage these projects. To many the Plan Organization must have seemed a foreign excrescence on the Iranian body politic.

The manner in which the Economic Bureau (later the Division) of the Plan Organization, with which the Harvard Group was to work, was organized and staffed did little to ameliorate this tinge of foreignness or to reconcile already estranged feelings in government ministries. There were very few trained economists in Iran. The few that were available had recently returned from foreign training, mainly in the United States, or were still abroad but might be induced to return to Iran. Among the inducements was a salary supplement offered by the Ford Foundation which provided an income substantially above ordinary Civil Service salaries. No doubt this was a questionable practice. But it provided at least a temporary solution to a problem that has confronted governments in many other developing countries—how to attract exceptionally able people, who could not be moved by ordinary civil service salaries, to posts that were deemed of exceptional importance. Certainly an unusually able group of young Iranian economists was attracted. They later went on to leading positions in government and business. Two of them became directors of the Plan Organization. There were, moreover, additional characteristics that set this group apart from other government officials on the same level. Most of them came from upper–class families accustomed to sending their sons and daughters abroad for education. This was not true of run–of–the–mill civil servants. Some of the former group had spent long periods abroad and, in the process, had acquired foreign wives and a distinctly western set of values.

It was in fact a group of exceptionally able young Iranians and foreign advisors who staffed the Economic Bureau. The head of the Bureau was Khodadad Farmanfarmaian, who later held a number of important positions in the Iranian Government. The Harvard field supervisor was Kenneth Hansen, an able and aggressive leader. So long as the tasks assigned the Bureau were primarily technical, appraising Plan Organization projects, preparing prospectuses for foreign investment institutions, and the like, no one else in Iran could do it better or, indeed, as well. The first large task undertaken by the Bureau, the 1959 Program Review, provided a highly useful survey of the state of Plan Organization projects and projections of future cash flows and requirements. But the Program Review also made clear that Plan Organization projects were not very well articulated with a sensible overall development program and that much had to be done before such a program was possible.

The 1959 Program Review coincided with a financial crisis which laid bare the deficiencies of Iran's financial management and brought the International Monetary Fund onto the scene. A weak Ministry of Finance limited its function to the raising of revenue and there was no central agency to exercise control over government expenditures. As a result various ministries borrowed abroad on their own authority and the accumulation of short–term debt set the stage for the crisis. Obviously, effective financial management in Iran required something in the nature of a budget bureau to scrutinize proposed public expenditures and closer cooperation among the Ministry of Finance, the Central Bank, and the principal investment agency, the Plan Organization. Furthermore, if financial management was to be properly articulated with the development process, something like a comprehensive plan seemed to be necessary. Ebtehaj held this view and was not only willing but anxious to see the Plan Organization play a leading role. The Second Plan period was to end in September 1962, and fifteen months before that date the High Economic Council, chaired by the Shah, assigned the Plan Organization this responsibility. A letter from the Prime Minister indicated that the Economic Bureau would be expected to be the central working group. In fact this was the only group in Iran with the technical competence needed for such a task.

Unfortunately, comprehensive planning, if it is to have a significant relation to what happens, requires more than technical competence. It requires a body of empirical data not available in Iran and a degree of cooperation among policy–making and administrative agencies of government that the Economic Bureau was not in a position to command. A distinguished development economist, Wolfgang F. Stolper, on the basis of his experience in Nigeria, has written a book called *Planning Without Facts*. No doubt, sensible recommendations with respect to general development priorities can be made without many facts, but even Stolper would admit that empirical investigation is needed to put flesh on what otherwise are rather bare bones.

As indicated above, Ebtehaj had been willing to finance numerous surveys that had provided the Plan Organization with new information on various sectors of the economy. When Ebtehaj was dismissed and replaced by his subordinate, however, these surveys were discontinued. The Economic Bureau, moreover, found great difficulty in securing cooperation from the various ministries whose assistance was essential. As George Baldwin, one of the Harvard advisors, observed:

> One of the most difficult and discouraging aspects of Iranian planning was the lack of interest shown by most Ministries in working up project proposals for consideration by the planning agency. . . . Instead of screening proposals made by "applicants" Plan Organization spent much of its time trying to generate specific proposals for inclusion in the Third Plan.[5]

He goes on to note that the projects that were in fact included either came mainly from the Plan Organization itself or "were those which had been contracted out to foreign consulting firms, such as the future road program, the Kuzestan regional program and a few others."

The author of those quotations, George Baldwin, was a member of the first Harvard team and his book is a good discussion of planning in Iran as seen by a member of that team. The field supervisor of the second team, which was in Iran during 1960–62, was a Canadian, Thomas H. McLeod. The first team, though with some doubts and misgivings, had nevertheless embarked rather enthusiastically on the preparation of a comprehensive plan and were sobered by the experience. The second team, condemned to live in a "world they had never made," grew progressively more sober as the Plan Organization lost prestige and influence after the departure of Ebtehaj, and relations with government ministries worsened.

Despite these difficulties the Third Seven–Year Plan covering the years 1962–69 was completed and published. No one has ever claimed that it had much to do with guiding the development of Iran during the following years. Before the Plan was published it was the judgment of two Danish economists who were members of the second Harvard group "that while the attempt to launch a comprehensive plan would undoubtedly fail, the drawing up of the Plan affected, irreversibly, the thinking of many people in government."[6] Perhaps this is the most that could be said of an effort of this sort. Something like this seems to have been the experience of many developing countries in early efforts at planning. From this beginning, either they have created planning commissions that were effectively integrated into the machinery of government and exerted some influence on development policies and public investment or else the practice of planning has been discredited. In Iran the Plan Organization, after experiencing a period of decline, again emerged as an important agency, but one more concerned with planning in the traditional sense than with the undertaking of investment projects on its own authority. But my connection with the Plan Organization ended in 1962 and I have not followed closely its later development, which, in any case, was brought to an abrupt end by the revolution in 1979.

With the benefit of hindsight it is possible to make a few observations on this Iranian experience.

The first concerns the relations between advisors and counterparts.[7] The first Harvard project director, Kenneth Hansen, was an entrepreneurial type who had had considerable experience in the American government and came to the project from a position as economist in a large oil company. He brought with him an exceptional, competent group of advisors, mainly American. His conception of the job was to do what needed to be done without much regard for the formal locus of authority. He was aided and abetted by Ebtehaj, who was primarily interested in expert advice rather than institution building and who developed a close personal relation with Hansen. A favorable result of this situation was that the Economic Bureau quickly established its position in the Plan Organization and was heavily relied on. If the Iranian counterparts had been a group of unimpressive civil servants, this situation might have gone on indefinitely with the advisors doing most of the work and giving little advice or training. But, in fact, the Iranian members of the Economic Bureau were an exceptionally talented group who learned rapidly in spite of a lack of special training efforts. Khodadad Farmanfarmaian, the director of the Economic Bureau, in a report to the Ford Foundation prepared after the conclusion of the project, characterized the work of the first group of advisors as follows. He said the Harvard group supervised by Hansen

> did a large part of the actual work of the Bureau. They made a lot of decisions, i.e., the Management of the Bureau, or the Iranian heads of Sections accepted decisions proposed by them, and they pushed, prodded, imposed and interfered. But at no time were the rights of the Iranians in charge of the sections in the Bureau to veto, reverse, and modify decisions ever violated.[8]

Elsewhere in his report, Farmanfarmaian estimates that in the first year perhaps 70 percent of the Bureau's decisions were made by the advisors, but in the last year of the first contract this had been reduced to perhaps 30 percent.

Hansen left in 1961 to accept a position as Assistant Director of the U.S. Bureau of the Budget under David Bell. His successor as director of the Harvard Advisory Group under the renewal contract, Thomas McLeod, was a senior financial official of the Government of Saskatchewan.[9] In the second round, most of the advisors were non–Americans, including three Scandinavians. McLeod's conception of his role was quite different from Hansen's. He regarded himself solely as an advisor and this was the position taken by his colleagues. And by this time a purely advisory role was wholly appropriate since the Iranian staff of the Bureau were by then relatively experienced officials.

This question of the appropriate role of advisors in the initial stage of a new organization is a difficult one. If their counterparts are inexperienced it is possible that, unless the advisors step out of a purely advisory role, the organization will never get off the ground. On the other hand, if they push too hard, they may not leave behind them an effectively functioning unit. In the Iranian case, there is no doubt that Hansen and his colleagues departed rather far from their role as advisors. But the situation was saved by the fact that their counterparts were an exceptionally able group of men who were not to be pushed aside.

A second observation concerns the relation of a planning unit to the other ministries and departments of government. As I have indicated, the Second Plan in Iran consisted solely of a number of projects and the Plan Organization was more of a public works agency than a comprehensive planning organization. In 1958, it commanded a sizable fraction of Iran's oil revenues, was able to borrow from the World Bank and other sources, and had the full support of the Shah. In these circumstances, it felt little need to cultivate other branches of government and, in fact, used them mainly as executing agencies for a number of its investment projects.

This position, however, was not conducive to the effective formulation and implementation of a comprehensive development plan. Although the Iranian members of the Economic Bureau and the advisors made great efforts to engage other ministries and departments in the planning effort, their success was spotty. And, although the Third Plan was formally accepted by government, there was not the follow–through that would have required the active participation of development ministries. This failure of the Economic Bureau to engage the active support of relevant agencies was, in large part, due to the declining prestige of the Plan Organization after the fall of Ebtehaj. He was succeeded by a series of weak managing directors, the share of oil revenues accruing to the Plan Organization continued to fall as other ministries asserted their claims, and the support of the Shah dwindled. By 1962, a number of leading officials in the Plan Organization had resigned, and the Economic Bureau lost its leader and the best of the Iranian staff to other branches of government. The second Harvard contract came to an end in September 1962, and both the Plan Organization and Harvard were quite content to see relations severed.

The Ford Foundation evaluation of the Iranian project was inclined to mark it down as a partial failure. In the judgment of Rey Hall, the Foundation representative in Iran,

> "The assignment of advisors through Harvard University, administered through IIE (Institute for International Education), had its supervisory and administrative deficits. It did support, effectively, the development of a creative and enthusiastic Iranian staff, although only partial success in the establishment of a cohesive planning unit was realized owing to indifferent government support and the lessening influence of the Plan Organization."[10]

Judged as an effort in institution building and viewed from the perspective of 1962, there was much to be said for this view.

The Plan Organization was weaker in 1962 than it had been in 1958 and the Iranian staff of the Economic Bureau, built up with considerable difficulty, was dispersed. From a broader and longer point of view, however, there is something to be said on the other side. The Economic Bureau and its advisors in their evaluation of the projects, in the preparation of proposals for the World Bank and other lenders, and in the analysis of budgets, introduced techniques that were relatively unknown in Iran and some of this outlived the departure of the advisors. Although the principal staff members of the Economic Bureau had left by the end of 1962, or departed shortly thereafter, they left for other positions in government where their training was useful. Two of them, Farmanfarmaian and Majidi, later became managing directors of a revitalized Plan Organization. And, although the preparation of the Third Plan may well have been premature, the effort had considerable influence on the preparation of later plans.

Teaching and Research

During the period before the formation of the Development Advisory Service, there was not much feedback to Harvard from the overseas projects. The Center for International Affairs brought George Baldwin, a member of the first Iran group, to Cambridge for the year 1960–61, when he began preparing the volume on planning referred to earlier. Other members of the Iran project later published studies on their experiences. On Pakistan, a spate of writing and publishing began in the 1960s.

The earlier teaching at Harvard in the field of economic development was not undertaken by people connected with the Pakistan or Iran projects. A one–semester undergraduate course on the Economy of China was given in 1950–51 by Dr. Douglas Paauw and he later added one on Japan and Southeast Asia. A one–semester undergraduate course on Theories and Problems of Economic Development was offered in 1954–55 by Assistant Professor Robert Baldwin, and this was continued for a number of years. In 1955–56 a full course (undergraduate) was offered by Dr. A. J. Meyer on the Economics of the Middle East, and he later added a graduate seminar on the same subject. In the same year, Professor John K. Galbraith offered a half–year graduate seminar on Economic and Political Development. This was later extended to a full year and when Bell and Papanek returned from Pakistan in 1958 they joined him in this seminar. I began my teaching in this area in 1959–60 with a seminar in Economic and Political Development in which I was joined by Galbraith, Bell, and Papanek. This seminar was designed in part for the Public Service Fellows who first came to Harvard in 1957–58. The seminar drew substantially on the Pakistan and Iran experiences; but extensive use of material from overseas projects came later.

2. The Second Stage: The Development Advisory Service

When the Center for International Affairs began operations in 1958–59, I became a half-time member of its faculty, teaching the Center's seminar in economic development, directing its research program in that area, and managing the overseas projects in Iran and Pakistan. I was assisted in managing these projects by David Bell until 1961, when he left to become Director of the Bureau of the Budget in the Kennedy Administration, and by Gustav Papanek. By the early 1960s a number of requests for advisory assistance had come in from other countries and the Ford Foundation was receiving many more. The Foundation was reaching for an outside instrument to which it could delegate some of these tasks. Harvard's experience in Pakistan and Iran suggested that such an instrument might be found in Cambridge. The result was the formation of the Development Advisory Service (DAS) in May 1962.

The Foundation assisted the DAS with a grant of $750,000, of which $550,000 was earmarked for the creation of a new type of university appointment to be known as Development Advisor.

> Men holding these appointments are committed to a career spent partly at Harvard and partly in underdeveloped countries. The terms of employment are intended to attract high–caliber professionals to long–term service. Appointments are made for a period of indefinite duration and entitle the holders to all the normal benefits of tenure appointments. It is understood that if the University decides to terminate the arrangement, an Advisor is entitled to 18 terminal months at Harvard, to be devoted to research or teaching.[11]

The grant contemplated financing ten Development Advisors but the DAS was never able to fill this many posts. The original group numbered four.[12] Many others in the overseas groups were called advisors, but Development Advisors had a special status.

By June 1963, the DAS had accepted responsibility for five projects. Three of these were designed to assist planning organizations in Pakistan, Colombia, and Argentina; while two were intended to assist research organizations: the Indonesian Institute of Economic and Social Studies (LEKNAS), in the Indonesian Ministry of National Research, and the Di Tella Institute in Argentina, a private, nonprofit organization. All five projects were financed by the Ford Foundation. With the exception of LEKNAS and the Di Tella Institute, they were headed by members of the newly–formed group of Development Advisors at the DAS:

> The operation of the Service, it is anticipated, will serve three purposes. It will fill certain critical needs of foreign governments and institutions concerned with economic development. It will add to the supply of trained professionals who have first–hand experience with the problems of developing nations. And it will enrich the teaching and research conducted at Harvard University on the subject of economic development.[13]

The first Director of the DAS was Professor Raymond Vernon, of the Harvard Graduate School of Business Administration, who had recently completed a study of the economic development of Mexico, under the sponsorship of the Center. He was expected to devote half–time to this assignment and he served for three years, 1962 to 1965. Gustav Papanek, who was Deputy Director under Vernon, became Director for the period 1965 to 1970, when he was succeeded by Lester Gordon. I served as Chairman of the Faculty Advisory Committee until my retirement in 1969.

From the beginning, the DAS adopted policies that were followed consistently throughout the life of the institution.

One important policy was that DAS teams should be multinational in order to avoid any impression that they were agents of U.S. foreign policy. For most of the projects most of the time, the number of non–Americans exceeded the number of Americans. In 1963–64, for example, the first full year of DAS operation, 38 professional staff served overseas, including 22 advisors and 16 short–term consultants. Of these 38 people, 18 were American, 7 British, 4 Norwegian, 2 Australian, 2 Dutch, 1 French, 1 Belgian, 1 Burmese, 1 Swedish, and 1 Brazilian. Although for the whole period of DAS operations, 1962–1974, there were (including consultants) slightly more Americans than foreigners, on the whole this guiding principle was well maintained.

A second policy was that no direct financing could be accepted from the U.S. Agency for International Development or any other bilateral program.

The rationale for this again was to avoid any suspicion of U.S. or other national influence. The importance of this policy was emphasized by the fact that, at least in early years, AID insisted on a security check for all its contract personnel. Although DAS accepted AID grants for research conducted in Cambridge, no overseas projects were financed directly by AID.

A third DAS policy was to insist on a team approach. This had worked well in Pakistan and Iran, and was followed in almost all projects. This method of providing advisory services has, however, been subject to criticism. It has been charged that the team device may lead to ambiguities in the line of command and responsibility. Is the advisor working for the government to which he has been assigned, for Harvard University, or possibly for the donor agency? This possible ambiguity has not, in fact, loomed large in DAS experience. A responsibility of the team leader was to make sure that all advisors considered themselves to be working with their counterparts for the host government. And there were advantages both in recruitment and in overseas operations in having a mutually supporting group of advisors. The alternative to a team approach is direct hire, either by the employing government or recruitment through some intermediary such as a donor agency. There is no doubt that direct hire may be preferable in certain circumstances, but the team approach has much to be said for it.

From the formation of the DAS in 1962 until it was succeeded by HIID in 1974, the institution administered some 17 projects in 14 countries. In ten of these countries, the DAS assisted in the formation and development of planning agencies.[14] The other projects were principally concerned with research assistance. During this period there were over 300 advisors and consultants overseas from the United States and 25 other countries. Providing this many bodies required an extensive recruiting effort and by 1970 the credentials of some 3,500 possible candidates had been evaluated. Many of the people who had served in DAS missions were later employed by the World Bank, AID, and other development institutions. The total dollar expenditures during this 12–year period were a little over $20 million. Of this, the Ford Foundation supplied slightly more than $10 million. The other large financial contributor was the United Nations Development Programme. Smaller amounts were contributed by the World Bank, the Inter–American Development Bank, and host countries themselves—whose dollar contributions came usually from loans and grants from the World Bank or USAID. Host countries also contributed substantial amounts of local currency and, of course, provided administrative services, domestic travel, and office accommodations.

The administration of these overseas programs required a sizable Cambridge staff to supply backstopping and monitoring services, undertake recruitment, and oversee the training program for foreign government officials studying at Harvard and at other universities under DAS auspices. In 1973–74, the last year of the DAS, there were, in addition to the Director, associate and assistant directors in charge of finance, research, recruitment, and training. In Cambridge also were some 12 research associates and research assistants, a number of whom taught courses in economic development. DAS and HIID overseas advisors have been able to rely extensively on staff work in Cambridge. In contrast, for example, to United Nations advisors who, in the field, are largely on their own, DAS and HIID advisors have been backstopped by an active home office staff and the resources of the University. During the same year, four research fellows and four consultants were at work on a public works study financed by the World Bank.

The multiproject operation with its Cambridge component brought certain economies of scale. The Development Advisors usually worked in more than one country and, in their periods in Cambridge, had an opportunity to reflect on and write about their experience. Increasingly, moreover, recruits for one mission signed on to work in other countries. The Acting Director of the Center for International Affairs, in the agency's report for 1965–1966, said of the DAS field projects in that academic year:

> Some 4 long–term advisors had been on the Harvard faculty, 6 had served with the DAS before, and 6 permanent Development Advisors were in the field. Of the 22 short–term consultants, 15 had an affiliation with Harvard, other than the DAS, most of them on the faculty; 7 had served with the DAS before. Clearly, the DAS is more and more drawing on University resources and is transferring experience from one project to another.[15]

And the Ford Foundation in its evaluation of the DAS in 1971, under the heading of "economies in scale and learning by doing," declared that

> the value of the DAS to its sources of financial support and to other international agencies concerned with providing foreign aid and technical assistance has been considerable. Its field teams have introduced elements of creativity, rationality, and analysis into development planning and project evaluations that have improved substantially the basis for aid decisions. Moreover, the university

setting of the DAS has enabled it to perform its administrative, recruiting and backstopping responsibilities in ways that donors could not easily duplicate.[16]

Pakistan: The Later Years

The Pakistan project was the largest, probably the most successful, and certainly the longest in DAS experience. In fact, it lasted too long as we shall see presently. What are the tests of performance in projects of this sort? Six seem to be relevant.

1. Acceptance of advice on policies which, when implemented, make an obvious contribution to the development of the country in question.
2. Assistance in building an institution that lives beyond the life of the project.
3. Training counterparts who are later influential either in the planning institution or elsewhere in the government.
4. Selection of people for training overseas who later become useful government officials.
5. Translating experience into publications useful in the literature of economic development.
6. Accumulation of experience relevant to other development programs, to other foreign assistance agencies, and to teaching.

By all these tests, the Pakistan project must be judged a success, although there are qualifications.

As we have seen earlier, in the 1950s the Harvard Advisory Group labored under difficulties with rapidly changing governments, none of which showed much interest in economic development. Pakistan was that way. So far as one can judge from the inadequate statistics, national income grew in real terms at about 2 to 2½ percent a year, which was less than the rate of population growth. With imports from India excluded and manufactures from other sources under high protection, industry in Pakistan grew rapidly, about 15 percent a year during this period, but from a very low base. High domestic prices for manufactured products turned the terms of trade sharply against agriculture, and a heavily overvalued rupee handicapped exports.

All this began to change in 1958 when General Ayub Khan, in a bloodless coup, overthrew his predecessor, Iskander Mirza, and introduced military government. Although constitutional changes and an election of sorts made Ayub president in 1962, it was a very attenuated democracy that followed. But the Ayub regime, while maintaining law and order, was also strongly interested in economic development. The president was also interested in effective planning and in strengthening the Planning Commission, of which he became titular chairman.

In 1960, Richard Gilbert became Director of the Harvard Advisory Group and the head of a large and able group of advisors in Karachi, Lahore, and Dacca. Gilbert was not only a first–rate economist, but strongly policy–oriented. He was helped by the fact that an able Minister of Finance, Mohammed Shoaib, later vice–president of the World Bank, worked closely with the Planning Commission. Clear evidence of a turnaround was visible by 1963. In his progress report to the DAS covering the period April 1963 to June 1964, Gilbert notes:

> The past year has witnessed a fundamental reappraisal, at home and abroad, of Pakistan's development program. In part because of better measurements of national output and its component sectors that have now become available, in part because of breakthroughs in production and exports unmistakable under any set of measurements, there has been literally a transformation in the image of Pakistan's development program, its performance, projects and management.[17]

In a memorandum to a consortium headed by the World Bank to provide external financing, it was noted that export earnings had increased during the Second Plan period by 7 percent per annum, that gross investment at 18 percent of GNP had doubled, and that GNP was increasing at the rate of 5 percent and was expected to reach 6 percent in the last year of the Plan, 1964–65. Perhaps the most remarkable change occurred in agriculture, particularly in West Pakistan. Although public policy had something to do with this via increased expenditure on irrigation and the moderation of price controls on agricultural products, the main impetus came from the installation of private tubewells which favored an optimum use of water supplies. This development also gave a pronounced impetus to industry through the domestic production of pipe and electric motors.

The Advisory Group also reached its maximum strength during this period, when there were 12 advisors and 6 consultants at the Planning

Commission in Karachi, 4 advisors and 1 consultant in Lahore, and 5 advisors and 1 consultant in Dacca. The staff in Karachi also included two training associates, Joseph Stern and Carl Gotsch. More important, the Pakistani staff of the Planning Commission greatly increased in size and improved in quality. The prestige of the Planning Commission was now sufficient to attract the best young economists in Pakistan. One of the ablest of these recruits was Mabul–ul–Haq, who has served as Minister of Finance and Minister of Planning in Pakistan.

By the end of the Second Plan period, the Planning Commission was effectively articulated with all the development agencies of Government, and served as the central economic staff. In his progress report for the period, January 1, 1966 to June 30, 1966, Gilbert wrote as follows:

> The Planning Commission has in recent years assumed a role of the most far–reaching proportions. It not only prepares the long–term plans, the Five–Year Plans, the Annual Development Programs, but has assumed a staff role to the Central Government on all economic policy issues and is deeply involved in all aspects of current economic operations. Representatives of the Planning Commission attend meetings of the National Economic Council, the Executive Committee of the NEC, the Cabinet, the Governor's Conferences, the Investment Promotion Bureau, the Heavy Industries Board, the Foreign Exchange Control Committee, indeed well nigh every governmental instrumentality with economic responsibilities.[18]

It is not too strong to say that during this period the Planning Commission of Pakistan was one of the most effective planning agencies in the less developed world—perhaps *the* most. But this happy situation was not to last. In his progress report, Gilbert had noted with some misgivings, "It is now decided policy that the Harvard project will terminate in June, 1965."[19] It is unfortunate that this decision was not carried out.

Before I turn to the later stages of the Pakistan Project, something needs to be said in general terms about the development policies of the government supported by the Planning Commission and the Harvard Advisory Group. The principal, if not the sole objective, was to increase national income as rapidly as possible. Little attention was paid to equitable distribution. As a progress report notes,

> As in the early stages of capitalism elsewhere, there are unlovely aspects in the growing inequalities of the distribution of income,

> property, and power, and growing tension in the urbanized and industrialized areas. Pakistan is aware of this mounting problem, but has chosen to run the risk of social discontent and perhaps worse, in the interests of speeding up the pace of development."[20]

Later these discontents and tensions were exploited by Z. A. Bhutto in his attacks on Pakistan's "twenty–two families," culminating in his political successes of the 1970s.

One measure, however, aiming at more equitable distribution, in which the Advisory Group had a large hand was the Rural Public Works program. This program, utilizing grain imported under America's PL 480 to feed unemployed workers and enable them to undertake local public works (roads, canal repairs, local markets, etc.), was, at least for a time, a great success, particularly in East Pakistan. At one stage 800,000 were employed in East Pakistan and public works of substantial merit were completed.[21] But, on the whole, the policy influence of the Planning Commission and the Advisory Group was directed toward liberalization of the economy with increased productivity as the objective. A Development Advisor, Joseph Stern, who spent a long period in Pakistan, notes that by current standards of liberalization not much was done. But, in contrast with India, the liberalization effort was significant. Substantial changes in foreign exchange policy, the substitution of indirect for direct controls, the elimination of requisitions of and price controls on agricultural products, and other moves toward freer markets were the objectives and, in the main, they were accomplished.[22]

A turn for the worse for the Planning Commission and the Advisory Group began in 1965 with the war with India. The U.S. cut off aid to both India and Pakistan, and when consortium assistance was restored in 1966, it was at a considerably lower level. Pakistan's military expenditures doubled and some of the liberalization measures of the early 1960s were put in doubt. Although GNP grew at the rate of 5 percent during the first two years of the Third Plan period, this was less than expected.

The influence of the Planning Commission was still high but the loss of prestige by President Ayub after the signing of the peace treaty at Tashkent in 1966 was rather rapidly transferred to the Commission. The Ford Foundation ceased financing the project in 1965, and hindsight suggests that the DAS should have gone home. Since I was still chairman of the Faculty Advisory Committee, I must bear part of the responsibility for inadequate foresight. But the Government of Pakistan pressed hard and the World Bank indicated a willingness to finance a continuation.

According to a memo from Gustav Papanek, then Director of DAS:

> When the Pakistan project was extended in 1965, with World Bank financing, there was a general agreement among the three parties concerned—the Government of Pakistan, the Bank, and DAS—that the project should continue until work on the Fourth Five-Year Plan is completed, that is, until 1970. However, the initial agreement was for three years only, in order to give everyone a chance for second thoughts.[23]

The Bank-financed project provided a small staff at the Center, two advisors in Lahore, and four advisors in Dacca. When Papanek visited the project in September 1967, he noted some anti-western feeling, a decline in the prestige of the Planning Commission, and increasing attacks on liberalization policies. But,

> in East Pakistan, the advisory group *is*, to a large extent, the Planning and Development Department. Their influence is great, and they are involved in practically all major economic decisions which affect the Province.[24]

Although he reported that relations between advisors and Pakistani colleagues were good, this is hardly the role that advisors would be expected to occupy ten years after the beginning of operations in East Pakistan.

The last two years of the project were financed by the United Nations Development Programme with the World Bank acting as executing agency and with assistance from USAID counterpart funds. It was a dismal period in all respects. Extensive urban riots countrywide led to the downfall of Ayub and a military takeover by General Yaya Khan in 1968. The role and prestige of the Planning Commission declined precipitously. The Commission in Lahore was dismantled as the province was divided into five subprovinces. Disputes between East and West Pakistan were already presaging a dismantlement of the Union, and protests against foreigners in the government were growing.

As George Rosen, in his study of Ford Foundation activities in India and Pakistan, summarized the situation,

> The Planning Commission and the Harvard Advisory Group, formerly associated with economic success, were now associated with the economic weakness of a government in which the Commission played a major role, while the Harvard Group played an important, visible advisory role. The Yaya Khan government

> was overthrown by popular unrest; the new military government wished to show both its independence of the past, and a greater distance from the United States. An easy way to do both, to weaken the Planning Commission and to satisfy nationalist critics of foreign influence, was to make things sufficiently uncomfortable for the Harvard Group so that it would leave.[25]

Bowing to the inevitable, the DAS discontinued the project in 1970, and by June 30 all the advisors were gone.

Other Overseas Planning Projects

I have discussed the Pakistan project at some length not only because it was the largest and longest–lived DAS venture but because it illustrates both the successes and failures of such projects. But there were nine other planning projects (including Iran) undertaken by the DAS with varying degrees of success. I consider them in the order of their initiation.

Argentina

Shortly after its formation the DAS, with financing by the Ford Foundation, undertook a three–year contract (January 1, 1963, to December 31, 1965) with the Government of Argentina to advise the National Development Council (Conade), a division of the Economics Ministry, and to help prepare a development plan. Richard Mallon was the project director, assisted by two advisors until June 1964, when a fourth member of the team was added. A number of short–term consultants were also employed including Simon Kuznets, Richard Heflebower, and Etienne Hirsch, formerly head of the Commissariat du Plan in France. Raymond Vernon, then Director of the DAS, made a number of visits to Argentina.

Conditions in Argentina in 1963 and 1964 looked promising for increased rationality in policymaking and planning. Conade was effectively integrated with the so–called Economic Group of development ministries and the Central Bank. The staff of Conade, though young and inexperienced, was vigorous and intelligent. The work of the advisors was mainly concerned with helping to improve the statistical base for policymaking, establishing working relations with development agencies, and preparing the framework for a development plan.

The Center for International Affairs' annual report for 1965–1966 was optimistic on DAS activities in Argentina:

> In the course of the year, significant progress was made in economic policy: the budget deficit was reduced; the foreign debt was serviced and a substantial sum repaid; the national product continued to increase at a rapid rate (about 7 percent). . . Although the picture was less favorable as regards incomes policy and measures to slow inflation, the general outlook was good.[26]

The first contract finished at the end of 1965 but the project continued on the basis of a commitment by the Inter–American Development Bank to finance Conade and a promise by Conade to undertake a contract with the DAS. But, as frequently happens in Argentina, the political situation was increasingly unstable and opposition to the government was mounting. In May 1966 the armed forces gave President Illia 100 days "to make a credible record" and then, on June 28, staged a coup. This occurred before Conade had signed the contract with DAS and, although the military government later honored the commitment, the position of the advisors was uncertain. General Onganía, a retired military officer who became head of state, discharged personnel in the two top levels of Conade and replaced most of the existing ministers. Although he replaced them mainly with civilians, there was no doubt this was a military government. According to the Fifth Annual Report of the DAS,

> The new authorities of the Council expressed an interest in retaining the DAS Advisory Group, but in view of the uncertainties and poor prospects for an improvement in the situation in the near future, it was jointly agreed to suspend the project.[27]

The last advisor left in January 1967.

Raymond Vernon, then Director of the DAS, who paid considerable attention to the Argentina project, was asked whether he thought the project had had any lasting influence on institutions and policies. On the basis of hindsight, he responded as follows:

> Although there was an exceptional group of advisors who wrote a series of useful papers for an intelligent director who himself had considerable influence in government circles, there is not much evidence that Argentina's development policies were affected.
>
> The advisors had little or no knowledge of the political trade–offs among various ministries and departments and their counterparts had too little experience to help them. The Argentine

> material, however, was analyzed and the results published in a series of effective articles and books and the accumulated experience was useful in other DAS projects.[28]

Richard Mallon, who was director of the project, expressed a more favorable evaluation:

> The main professional contributions the advisory group made to Argentine policy were the "crawling peg" exchange rate which was later credited with helping break the $1 billion export ceiling and the stabilization policy model of Maynard and van Rijckeghem. The latter was subsequently used by Economic Minister Krieger Vasena quite effectively. There were other significant contributions too, such as Simon Kuznets' improvement of the national accounts.
>
> But the most lasting effects of the project were on people rather than on rapidly changing institutions. The same people we worked with are now back in power again—let's see if they can do better this time.[29]

It should also be noted that the analysis of the Argentine economy written by Mallon and Sourrouille has since become a standard university textbook on Argentina.[30]

Colombia

The spring of 1963 saw the beginning of a three–year project in Colombia designed to help the Department of Planning (Planeación) and the Ministry of Finance to develop an effective mechanism for planning and implementation. Initially three or four advisors were to be recruited with a larger operation contemplated later. The first project director was Harold Dunkerley, an able English economist who later became a senior official in the World Bank. By temperament Dunkerley was much like Hansen, the first project director in Iran—a doer rather than advisor. He quickly established close relations with the Minister of Finance and accompanied him to meetings with consultative groups in Washington, D.C., undoubtedly a dubious practice for an advisor. Two other advisors, Bengt Metelius and Richard Bird, also spent more of their time with the ministry and the Junta Monetaria than with the Department of Planning.

The political situation in Colombia during the first project period was unstable and the position of Planeación uncertain. During much of this period it was without a director. The Harvard staff in Planeación devoted most of its attention to improving statistics and in working with the Budget Office on the annual budget. Colombia had a 10–year plan, 1962–1972, but it had little influence on government decision–making.

This situation changed markedly in 1966 with the election of President Lleras and the appointment of Edgar Gutiérrez as director of Planeación. With this improved outlook, discussions were initiated for an expanded advisory group and the Ford Foundation made a second three–year grant. President Lleras requested the preparation of a four–year plan to replace the outmoded ten–year plan and the staff of Planeación was greatly strengthened. As the Fifth Annual DAS Report (1966–67) observed, "The Planning Agency, previously in danger of disappearing, has been greatly strengthened, and plays a key role in economic management."[31]

Richard Mallon had replaced Dunkerly as project director, though for several months the project had been without a director. The period, 1966–1969, was one of expansion in Colombia as coffee prices rose; of growth in the size and quality of the Planeación staff; and of close cooperation by the DAS advisors on the principal issues of development policy. A constitutional amendment in 1968 had required Planeación to revise the Plan annually, each year rolling the projections forward by a year. On the occasion of the announcement by President Lleras of the Four–Year Plan, 1969–1972, Edgar Gutiérrez, retiring director of Planeación, remarked,

> The Four–Year Plan, by contrast, had been prepared by a Department whose staff was simultaneously involved in programming and evaluating day–to–day economic policies and public investments, so that the Plan projections do not go beyond a feasible evolution of the present situation.[32]

As of November 1969, Planeación had a staff of about 250 including 142 professionals and was certainly the leading planning agency in Latin America.

The Harvard Advisory Group in Colombia paid considerably more attention to training staff members than was true of most other DAS projects. Most advisors and consultants gave regular seminars in their specialties, and a number of advisors also taught courses at the University of the Andes, from which many of the staff of Planeación were recruited. This undoubtedly helped in working the DAS out of a job.

At the end of 1969, Jorge Luis Lara, former dean of the faculty of economics at the University of the Andes, became director of Planeación.

Clive Gray was now director of the Harvard project. On June 15, 1970, Misael Pastrana took office as president of Colombia and pledged continuity with the policies of the Lleras government, including support of Planeación. In the year 1969–70, the Ford Foundation provided 60 percent of the financial support of the project and the other 40 percent came from a loan to Colombia by the Inter–American Development Bank. The Bank had declared this to be a "one shot" operation but for some reason, undisclosed, both Planeación and DAS had expected it to be renewed and the Ford Foundation had set aside money for continued support of the project. When it became clear that the Bank meant what it said, Lara ordered a complete re–evaluation of the department's technical assistance needs. The evaluators generously praised the DAS contribution, but reached these principal conclusions:

1. In view of the greatly increased strength and technical competence of the DNP, it is no longer desirable to have a foreign advisory group led by its own director.
2. In–service training by foreign advisors should be phased out as rapidly as possible and assistance should be concentrated on highly specialized short–term or basic longer–term analysis and research.[33]

As Richard Mallon observed,

> The declaration of independence of the DNP is, of course, a healthy development. It also signifies that the DAS has been successful in working itself out of a job. This development, however, is occurring a year earlier and in a different manner than was being planned by the DAS.[34]

There were still contracts to run out, but by the end of 1971 all the DAS personnel had left Colombia.

Despite some awkwardness in terminating the project, the DAS venture in Colombia must, by any proper test, be considered a success. The DAS found a planning organization that was doubtful of survival and left one that was, in every respect, a thriving organization. It not only provided sound technical advice, but had a large hand in training a highly competent staff of civil servants.

A Ford Foundation appraisal of the project does not differ essentially from this estimate though it emphasizes a discrepancy between Foundation and DAS objectives that characterized most of these planning ventures:

> The Foundation looked upon the project as purely an educational venture (albeit in a non–academic setting), whereas the DAS and its advisors took a much more active position and used the opportunity for experimentation with new policies and programs. . .
>
> But in a field like economic policy and planning, it must be noted, it is difficult to draw a line between education and training and participation in policy formulation and implementation, when the setting in which training is conducted is in fact the setting in which policy is made for the country. . . Toward the end of the ten–year period, Colombian scholars became competent enough to begin to assert that they could handle problems as well as the expatriate scholars, a true test of the educational process implicit in the project.[35]

Liberia

The next planning project undertaken by the DAS was in Liberia. It was financed by the United Nations Development Programme for "an initial two years" to advise the newly formed National Planning Agency. As usual in UNDP contracts, Liberia was to cover 15 percent of the costs. The contract called for four or five advisors and a few consultants, and the first advisors arrived in Monrovia in the spring of 1964. The first project director was Elliot Berg of the University of Michigan, followed by William Hollinger, one of the core group of Development Advisors.

The Liberia project presented quite a new experience and a different set of development problems for the DAS. Liberia was by far the least developed country it had encountered. The government was disorganized and staffed by poorly trained civil servants. The Planning Department was an embryonic organization with five or six untrained counterparts. The Liberian economy and society were dualistic in the extreme. The descendants of American slaves (the Liberian–Americans) held all the positions of economic and political power and were congregated in Monrovia and a few towns along the coast. The rest of the country was occupied by tribes which had little contact with the quasi–modern economy. The country was rich in natural resources—iron ore, rubber, palm oil, timber, and most of the very high rate of investment (25–35 percent of GNP) came from concessions to exploit these resources. According to Papanek, the "President [Tubman] continues to run Liberia in a style which would be familiar to the princes of the Italian Renaissance."[36] Since he distributed the privilege of dealing with foreign concessionaires among his political favorites, this became a major difficulty in improving concession terms. Liberia was a prime example of that relationship between foreign investors and local representatives delineated by the "dependencia" theorists.

Since Liberia used the American dollar as its currency, monetary and foreign–exchange policies were of negligible importance. The budget was the central instrument of government policy, and much of the attention of the Planning Department was given to questions of taxation, borrowing, and expenditures. The DAS staff was also concerned with improving statistics, with studies of the banking system and the concessions agreements, and with the preparation of Liberia's first development plan. Perhaps the most important substantive contribution of the advisors was the production of recommendations on, and assistance in, negotiating concessions agreements. This was one of the specific functions assigned to the Planning Department in the legislative act which established it. Two consultants from Harvard, Louis Wells, Jr., of the Business School and David Smith of the Law School, had a large hand in this but a great deal of work was done by the staff of the Planning Department in collecting and analyzing concessions agreements, tax laws, and mining legislation from a large number of countries. The model concessions agreement worked out mainly by Wells and Smith was effectively used in later Liberian negotiations and had, perhaps, some influence in the concessions negotiations of other African countries.

The project was twice extended with UNDP financing and ended January 1, 1970. The last extension provided for three advisors from the DAS and three from the United Nations working under DAS management. Hollinger succeeded Elliot Berg as project director and during the final contract period the director was Carl Anonsen, a Norwegian from the Christian Michelsen Institute.

During the six years of the project, the staff of the Development Department was substantially increased and improved, and the position and prestige of the department in the government enhanced. By the middle of May 1968, in addition to the Secretary, two deputy secretaries, and the department counsellor, there were 12 professional staff members. In Papanek's opinion, "even without its foreign advisors, it would now be the strongest department in the government."[37] The first Secretary of the department, James Weeks, became Minister of Finance and his place was taken by an able administrator, Cyril Bright. The department worked closely with the Ministry of Finance on all questions of economic policy.

There is little doubt that advisors could have been used effectively after

1969, but several considerations worked against another renewal of the contract. The U.N. representative in Liberia was in favor of direct hire, and although his opposition to a DAS renewal might have been overcome, DAS recruiting for Liberia was difficult in any case. Besides, most of what could be learned had been learned, at least in the economic sphere.

There is no doubt that Monrovia was a difficult place for advisors. In the opinion of Vernon, the DAS missed an opportunity of studying an interesting and rapidly changing social environment but it is doubtful whether the Liberian government would have been interested in, or the UNDP willing to finance, such studies. On the whole, it would be my conclusion that the Liberian project was useful both to Liberia and to the DAS.

Greece

The next project undertaken by the DAS was at the opposite end of the development scale from Liberia. Indeed there was astonishment in certain quarters that a country as developed as Greece was thought to need advice. There is some evidence that the DAS was more concerned with what it could learn from the project than with what it could teach. And it was thought that recruiting for service in Greece would be an easy task.

The institution to be advised was the Center of Planning and Economic Research (KEPE), which was the outgrowth of a research organization established a number of years earlier by Andreas Papandreou to bring modern economic analysis to Greece. With a grant from the Ford Foundation he had brought a number of distinguished economists from the University of California and had assembled 10 or 12 Greek counterparts to work with them. Papandreou had soon turned his attention to political action and, in the last year of the California connection, the agency had changed its name from the Center for Economic Research to the Center of Planning and Economic Research. It was this apparent shift to a concern with economic policy analysis and advice that had attracted the DAS.

A grant from the Ford Foundation effective September 1966 was designed to finance a staff of four to five advisors and a number of consultants. The project director, Stephen Triantis, a Canadian of Greek extraction, arrived during the summer to prepare the way for this team. The purpose of the DAS project with KEPE was to help create, in the span of four or five years, a self–sufficient institution which could serve the Ministry of Coordination as its key source of economic policy analysis, improve the performance of its traditional research function, and help it become a leading center for graduate training in economics.

The emphasis on policy analysis assumed that the government then in power wanted such assistance. But, according to a memorandum from Lester Gordon, who visited Greece in June 1967:

> As early as the end of 1966 it had become apparent to the DAS that the coalition government then in power was so fully occupied with the problems of simply remaining in office that it was incapable of seriously addressing the policy problems of Greek economic life.[38]

An earlier memo from Papanek noted:

> The Center of Planning and Economic Research plays a small role in economic policy formulation. It has concentrated on filing requests for analysis and recommendations on relatively unimportant issues referred to it by the Ministry of Coordination and on revising a plan that is not particularly significant in shaping government decisions.[39]

Still, according to Papanek,

> The decision to undertake the project appears sound. We should be able to learn a good deal from the Greek project.

Papanek went on to advise the DAS that,

> Since the Center is not too well equipped to advise on current economic policies and since, in any case, the government is unlikely to use much advice, it will be desirable to concentrate on strengthening the Center so that it is able to provide advice when there is a government better able to take advantage of it.[40]

This redefined purpose of the project continued to be accepted until the coup of the "colonels" initiated a military government in April 1967. A second advisor, P. D. Henderson, had followed Triantis to Greece in February 1967, but it was now decided to do no more recruiting "until the dust had cleared." The dust cleared rather slowly so far as the DAS was concerned. The colonels imprisoned Papandreou and a number of other Greek leaders, dismissed the head of the Center, George Coutsamaris, and abrogated civil liberties. At the same time, a group of eminent Greek lawyers were appointed to write a new constitution and many people thought a civilian government might soon be restored.

Triantis was due to leave the project on September 1, 1967, and the DAS advisory committee in Cambridge had tentatively decided to end the project at that time. In July 1967, I spent ten days in Greece. The day before I arrived Thanos, the Secretary General of the Ministry of Coordination, had met with the Center's staff and assured them that the Ministry of Coordination expected to work closely with them. Still a number of the abler staff people were obviously looking for jobs abroad.

I arranged a meeting with Prime Minister Kolias, the King's man in the cabinet, and asked him how he thought events would develop. He said that the Constitutional Commission would report at the latest in November. After the military government had studied the draft they would, assuming they approved, submit it to a plebiscite for ratification. After that its provisions would be put into effect by stages. Political parties would have to be reconstituted, and freedom of the press, speech, assembly, etc., would be restored by degrees.[41]

After consultation with the DAS advisors, Coutsamaris, and the Greek staff of the Center, I wrote to Papanek as follows:

> The essential problem confronting the DAS is whether we should reconsider our decision to terminate the project in September on the ground that this is a government with which we do not wish to work. The alternative would be to maintain a presence on the ground that the Center is an institution worth preserving and one that promises to be of use when and if the present Greek government moves in the direction of civilian control. After talking with Coutsamaris, Henderson, and the Greek staff members, there was no doubt in my mind that if Harvard were to sever connections now it would be a serious blow to the continued existence of the Center.[42]

The DAS decided to stay on, and this decision, on the basis of hindsight, was a serious mistake. The situation became worse not better. Henderson was the only advisor to continue, maintaining what was essentially a watching role. On December 4, 1967, when a considerable number of the Greek staff were leaving the Center, he wrote as follows:

> I would say that there is not the slightest reason for Harvard to revise in any respect its first reactions of dismay and disgust at the military government of Greece. The repression is as tight as ever, and indeed the scope of purges and repressive control has been steadily extended over time.[43]

On the basis of this judgment, the DAS decided to discontinue the project, and Lester Gordon went to Greece in January to deliver a letter to the Ministry of Coordination indicating that Harvard expected to end it on February 15. The letter indicated as reasons for termination various repressive actions by the Greek government. This elicited a fiery response from the ministry terminating the project at once and condemning the DAS and all its works. Again, on the basis of hindsight, the DAS should either have publicized its reasons with considerable fanfare or have eliminated the criticism. The Ford Foundation was annoyed at the way the Greek project was terminated. It felt, with some reason, that it should have been consulted about the letter from Harvard. As it was, the project ended in rather messy fashion.

The Greek project was in every sense a failure. Perhaps the DAS learned something from it but not what it expected to learn.

Ghana

The coup of February 1966 which deposed Kwame Nkrumah, President of Ghana, was undertaken by a military group cooperating with the police. The new government, calling itself the National Liberation Council, was without experience in civil administration and badly in need of economic advice. It turned to the Ford Foundation and the DAS and, on a preliminary visit in December 1966, the then Director, Gustav Papanek, found the situation ripe for an advisory mission:

> The outlook for a successful project is good. The government is relatively stable. The top economic policymaker [E. N. Omaboe, Chief Secretary, Ministry of Economic Affairs] is competent, and the government is particularly receptive to foreign advisors.[44]

There was little in the way of staff for economic policy research but Papanek thought the material was available.

A three–year grant was made by the Ford Foundation and a contract signed with the Ghanaian Government in February 1967 providing for 17 man–years of advisors, 3 man–years of consultants, and 6 man–years of graduate fellowships for Ghanaian economists. Three consultants were sent to Ghana early in 1967 and they were followed in August by the project director, Jozeph Koopman, a Dutch economist with considerable experience in LDCs. By early 1968, the project was in full swing.

The Ghana in which Kwame Nkrumah assumed power in 1956 was a relatively open, market economy, predominantly agricultural with cocoa exports accounting for 60–70 percent of foreign–exchange earnings. Nkrumah was a nationalist and a socialist who believed that Ghana could achieve political and economic independence only by a thoroughgoing restructuring of the economy. Industrialization and the "big push" were what was called for, and indeed these were measures commonly recommended in the current development literature. He was advised by leading development economists, W. Arthur Lewis, Nicholas Kaldor, and Dudley Sears among them, and, in the preparation of the Seven Year Plan concluded in 1963, some 16 foreign consultants were involved.

During the last years of colonial rule, gross domestic product had been growing at the rate of about 5 percent a year. During the Nkrumah period this had fallen to around 2½ percent despite large investments financed by increased domestic savings and heavy borrowing abroad. At the beginning of his regime foreign–exchange reserves amounted to about $450 million; at the end not only were these reserves exhausted, but Ghana's foreign debt was around $500 million, mainly in short–term and medium–term suppliers' credits. Obviously something more than industrialization and a "big push" were required. Tony Killick calls this a period of modernization without growth.[45]

Public investment during the last years of the Nkrumah regime had consisted largely of (1) a number of prestige projects; stadia, superhighways, and a series of lavish buildings erected for a meeting of the Organization of African Unity—afterwards unused; (2) some 55 industrial enterprises financed largely by supplier credits, most of which were losing propositions and some not even able to meet operating costs; and (3) a series of state farms on land cleared by capital–intensive methods, operated by overstaffed and inefficient workers' brigades. Ghana had one of the highest capital–output ratios in the less developed world. Much of the time of successor governments, and the Harvard advisors, was given to renegotiating foreign debt and attempts to improve the functioning of the state enterprises:

> Between 1960 and 1965 about 80% of contracted foreign indebtedness was in the form of suppliers' credits. All the public sector manufacturing enterprises were financed this way.[46]

The National Liberation Council had, in the emergency, called on the International Monetary Fund, which had helped work out a stabilization program, devaluing the cedi (the Ghanian monetary unit), imposing debt ceilings, and organizing a consultative group to renegotiate debt and seek substantial balance–of–payments support. The IMF representative was Moeen Qureshi, who later became vice president of the World Bank and who had been the ablest Pakistani staff member in the early days of Harvard's Pakistan project. Until he left Ghana in the middle of 1968, Qureshi was the primary foreign advisor to the Government of Ghana.

Economic policy advice to the National Liberation Council was provided by a group chaired by E. N. Omaboe and consisting of representatives of the principal economic ministries and the Central Bank. By the end of 1967, he had a planning staff consisting of 18 young and inexperienced Ghanaian economists and the DAS advisors. Papanek, visiting Ghana in December 1967, considered that the advisors "will have to play a very active role during the initial period" and he went on to say:

> Such a role is desirable not only because some problems cannot wait until greater competence has been developed in the Ghanaian staff, but also because Omaboe and the Ministry must play an active role in economic policy discussions if they are not to decline in influence, access to information, and government support.[47]

As a matter of fact, the advisors played a more active role throughout the project than advisors would be expected to play, largely because of the deficiencies of the Ghanaian staff. Although the size of that staff had doubled by the end of the project, its quality had not improved. As Killick observed,

> The economic personnel employed in the Ministry of Finance and Planning are of generally indifferent calibre, morale is low and motivation weak. Among the reasons for this are low salaries, an absence of effective supervision and communication, a tendency to give the most interesting work to advisors, a training and promotion policy that emphasizes seniority rather than merit, and a skepticism about the utility of the work that is undertaken.[48]

The National Liberation Council regarded itself from the beginning as a caretaker government preparing the way for a return to civilian rule; consequently it was not inclined to undertake bold, and possibly unpopular, economic measures. It stopped the creation of new state–owned industrial enterprises and gave half–hearted attention to improving the performance of those already in existence; it canceled the program for state farms and gave lip service at least to increasing food production and assisting cocoa farmers; for the rest it was content to follow the lines of the stabilization policy laid out by the IMF. As a result the Ghanaian economy stagnated and unemployment increased.

The devaluation engineered by the IMF in 1967 was too little and too late. Consequently the cedi continued to be overvalued and the government found it necessary to maintain import controls, though they were somewhat relaxed. To prevent import controls from unduly raising the price of imported goods, it was felt expedient to maintain a fairly comprehensive system of price controls, though they were ill enforced. The impression both inside and outside Ghana was that the centralized, socialist regime of Nkrumah had been replaced by an approach to a market economy, but, as Killick shows, the approach was feeble and hesitant. The stabilization policy did put an end to the rash public investment expenditures of Nkrumah's last years but it did little to stimulate growth.

In an attempt to encourage growth, the Ministry of Economic Affairs produced a two–year development plan, largely written by the advisors, covering the period from mid–1968 to mid–1970. According to Project Director Koopman, it was a "transitional one intended as the forerunner of a more comprehensive development plan." It was not a "comprehensive blueprint" but a "broad analysis of the country's economic problems and a statement of the key policies which the government believes will be effective and can be implemented."[49] Among other objectives the two–year plan gave a high priority to agriculture; emphasized the necessity of utilizing existing industrial capacity and eliminating loss–making firms; improving infrastructure, mainly feeder roads; and overhauling the system of import licensing. But the rate of domestic savings continued to decline and, despite renegotiation and reduction of foreign debt, Ghana was during this period a capital–exporting rather than a capital–importing country.

As a result of elections, a new civilian government came to power on October 3, 1969, headed by Dr. K. A. Busia and his Progress Party. The Ministries of Finance and Economic Affairs were merged into the Ministry of Finance and Economic Planning under Minister J. H. Mensah, who had been the chief coordinator of Nkrumah's Seven Year Plan. He was served by two principal secretaries and Dr. Jones Ofari–Atta, the Junior Minister charged wtih economic planning, the portfolio which included the Harvard Advisory Project. A little later the Ford Foundation extended its grant for two more years until the middle of 1972. Koopman's position as director of the project was taken over by Walton Anderson, a Canadian agricultural economist, who was followed by Edward Shaw and then by Joseph Stern, a member of the central core of Harvard's Development Advisors.

The advent of the Busia regime had been greeted by many in Ghana and by the Advisory Group with hope and enthusiasm. And, during the first year, high cocoa prices offered some promise, although Papanek, visiting Accra in February 1970, complained,

> One can say about Ghana, as unfortunately about a number of other countries, that the government has so far shown little evidence that it knows what it wants to do in the economic sphere.[50]

The situation turned rapidly worse. Cocoa prices, which had averaged $930 a ton in 1969, fell to an average of $562 a ton in the first six months of 1971. Consumer prices, rising at 6 to 7 percent a year, decreased the international value of the cedi, which was already overvalued. While export earnings were declining, imports accelerated, responding to the strongly expansionist spending proposals in the budget of 1971–72. The "Economic Indicators" issued in June 1971 estimated that during 1971 export earnings would be about $325 million and imports would be about $485 million. The monthly issuance of the "Economic Indicators" was introduced by Tony Killick with contributions by other advisors. Joseph Stern believes that the dissemination of this information was perhaps the most important piece of work done by the advisors in Ghana, as these indicators were regularly considered at monthly meetings of the cabinet. Obviously a balance–of–payments crisis was approaching. The government was facing a choice among a return to thoroughgoing import licensing, a sharp rise in tariff rates, and devaluation. Consultation with London and Washington indicated that further financial assistance would not be forthcoming until the IMF had been called in. Although the IMF did not propose devaluation, it indicated that unless drastic measures were taken to improve the balance of payments, it could give no assistance. Faced with this solution, the government put a sharp devaluation into effect on December 27, 1971. Eighteen days later the government of Dr. Busia's Progress Party was overthrown in a military coup led by Colonel I. K. Acheampong.[51]

The value of the cedi in dollars before devaluation was $1.00 U.S. = ₵0.98 cedi. After devaluation the ratio was $1.00 U.S. = ₵0.55 cedi. The weighted average foreign–exchange price of the cedi fell 47 percent and the cedi price of foreign exchange rose 90 percent. The immediate result was a large increase in import prices and in some domestic prices exacerbated by a rather maladroit handling of the devaluation. The reactions to devaluation by the Ghanaian public provided an opportunity for the military that it had been waiting for. As Tony Killick, Michael Roemer, and Joseph Stern put it,

> The underlying causes of the coup had little to do with the devaluation, which merely presented the soldiers with an opportune moment to strike. In retrospect it is clear that the executioner's axe was already poised above Ghana's "democratic experiment": the most that a different set of policies might have achieved would have been to stay his hand for a little.[52]

Shortly after the takeover, Colonel Acheampong, addressing the staff of the Ministry of Finance and Planning, repudiated the Busia regime and all its works.

> The political frame of reference which has guided your actions and your advice, especially in the last two years, must be cast into the rubbish heap of history. This means a departure from the "laissez–faire" so–called market economy and the institution of effective planning in the allocation of resources.[53]

But, as Killick wryly observes, it cannot be said that market policies were a failure in the 1960s since market policies were never really tried.

The project continued to its termination in mid–1972 without effectively meshing with the new government. Based on the criteria I advanced earlier, it can hardly be described as a success. An exceptionally able group of advisors worked hard under unfavorable circumstances to provide economic advice to the Government of Ghana without notable achievement, and they did not train Ghanaians who later achieved prominence in government. Probably the most that can be said is that a few of them made substantial contributions to the development literature on Africa. The principal lesson to be derived from the experience is that unless a government gives high priority to economic development and is strong enough to carry out frequently unpopular measures to attain it, it is not going to develop, and a group of foreign advisors, no matter how able, can do little about it. The subsequent history of Ghana does not suggest that this lesson has been effectively learned.

Malaysia

The Harvard project in Malaysia began in 1966 when the DAS was asked to help strengthen the Economic Planning Unit (EPU) and help establish a Development Administration Unit (DAU), both of them in the Prime Minister's Department. Subsequently in 1968 assistance was extended to include an advisor for the economic division of the Treasury. The project was supported by a two–year grant from the Ford Foundation providing for 15 man–years of advisors and consultants. This grant was extended three times and the Foundation–supported project ended in 1975. Then, after a two–year hiatus, a small three–year advisory project was financed by the United Nations Development Programme. Harvard has had a long connection with Malaysia. Here we are concerned only with the nine years of advisory service from 1966 to 1975.

Malaysia had become independent in 1957 and the years from then until the DAS entered the scene had been rather stormy. They included the struggle, with British military assistance, against the Communist guerillas; the last British soldiers leaving in 1965. In 1963, Singapore, Sabah, and Sarawak were brought into the Malay Federation and the country became Malaysia. This expansion was strongly opposed by Indonesia and led to the "konfrontasi," which, for a time, threatened open warfare. Lee Kuan Yew's attempt to gain a share of power in Kuala Lumpur led to the expulsion of Singapore from the Federation in August 1965. During this period the civil service of Malaysia was rapidly Malayanized though as late as 1965, the EPU, which had been established in 1961, was directed by a foreigner from the United Nations.

The constitutional arrangements of 1957 bestowing citizenship on the Chinese, Indians, and other long–term inhabitants, had assured political control to the Malays. An implicit "handshake" pursuant to this agreement allowed the Chinese and foreigners, who owned and controlled most of the manufacturing, mining, and commerce in Malaysia, relative freedom from regulation while permitting the government to utilize public resources to promote the well–being of the Malay population. Thus the relationship among ethnic groups permeated the political, economic, and social life of Malaysia. As Milton Esman observed,

> Communal issues in Malaysia are so salient, interwoven into every issue of public policy and public management, that they must be explicitly calculated in every policy decision.[54]

Furthermore, the ethnic structure of Malaysia dictated that not only growth but equity must be the objective of development policy. Donald Snodgrass, a DAS advisor with previous experience in Malaysia, noted that Malaysia was in a better position than most other LDCs to tackle the issue of income distribution:

> Malaysia's political system, far from suppressing the distribution issue, has brought it to the fore. The fiscal system, which by the late 1960s was collecting 26–27 percent of GDP as government

> revenue (including Employees' Provident Fund contributions), is relatively well developed.[55]

Central issues of development, therefore, were how much revenue could be collected by taxation, largely paid by Chinese and foreign–owned enterprises, and how it could best be allocated to the benefit of the Malay population.

Malaysia had had a certain experience with economic planning before the advent of the DAS team. A rudimentary plan consisting of a number of investment projects had been prepared for the period 1950 to 1955. But the great impetus to comprehensive planning was given by a World Bank survey mission in 1954. According to Snodgrass, the Bank mission

> made a number of important institutional recommendations which were subsequently acted upon and prepared an investment programme which became the Federation's first real development plan.[56]

A planning secretariat, which later became the EPU, was established and a separate development budget was instituted. A second Five–Year Plan covered the period 1961–1966. The EPU was advised from 1964 through 1966 by a direct–hire team from the Ford Foundation, of which Snodgrass was a member. By the time the DAS appeared on the scene, the Federation of Malaya had become Malaysia and the EPU was engaged in preparing the first Malaysian Five–Year Plan.

From an organizational point of view, the Economic Planning Unit was well situated to influence the formation of economic policy. It reported directly to the Deputy Prime Minister, Tun Abdul Razak, the strong man in the Malaysian government, who was later to become Prime Minister. It served as a secretariat for the Economic Committee of the Cabinet and the National Development Council. The EPU was also well represented on the principal economic policy committees of government. On the other hand, apart from the director, Thong Yaw Hong, a civil servant of Chinese descent, the staff of the EPU was composed of young and relatively inexperienced personnel. As a result, the Harvard advisory group found itself doing more of the work than advisors should ideally be expected to do. The first DAS project director was William Gates, a professor of economics from Williams College. The second was Just Faaland, a Norwegian, director of research at the Christian Michelsen Institute. He was followed by Vincent Barnett, a professor of government at Williams. The last director was Paul Clark, also a professor of economics at Williams.

As indicated earlier, the Malaysia project also called for providing an advisor to the Development Administration Unit (DAU). In 1965, at the request of Tun Razak, the Ford Foundation had financed a two–man mission composed of Professor John Montgomery of Harvard and Milton Esman of the University of Pittsburgh to prepare a report on needed administrative reform. This report which, among other things, recommended the formation of the DAU, was accepted by Razak and the cabinet and published by the Government of Malaysia.[57] Razak was principally concerned with improving the implementation of development policies. Esman, the first senior advisor to the DAU, reported as follows on Razak's speech to the staff of the unit:

> He is concerned that the present bureaucracy, sluggish, lazy, overstaffed, underemployed, in general is not producing the output which the country. . . requires.[58]

The DAU, under a competent director, got off to a good start and for a while its reports went regularly to the cabinet for consideration. Its subsequent career, however, was checkered and like so many administrative units in less developed countries, its success or failure depended on the presence or absence of a single energetic and competent individual. It was converted in December 1971, through a merger with the implementation and coordination units, into ICDAU (Implementation and Coordination Development Administration Unit), but this did not notably improve its performance. The DAS provided a number of advisors, none of whom considered himself to be effectively employed. When I visited Kuala Lumpur in 1972, the DAU advisor was Hamlin Robinson, an able man, who kept busy on his own work program, relatively independent of the agency to which he was attached.

As for the Economic Planning Unit (EPU), the staff and the advisors were fully employed in preparing multi–year plans and annual development budgets, conducting sectoral surveys, providing secretarial services to the various development commissions, and backstopping negotiations with international lending agencies. The subject areas to which the advisors were assigned were industry, manpower and employment, agriculture, project analysis and capital budgeting, and macroeconomic planning. The advisors also undertook a substantial amount of staff training, giving a course in mathematical economics and regular seminars in development economics. By the end of the first project this training, plus continuous recruitment, had resulted in a substantial upgrading of the Malaysian staff.

Malaysian agriculture, which was the principal concern of public investment, was divided into three segments: 1) the plantations (rubber and palm oil), which were mainly in the hands of foreigners; 2) smallholders producing for export; and 3) peasant producers and fishermen. The Malay segment of the population was predominantly in the third category, although there were Malays in the second category as well. The development expenditures of the government attempted to stimulate productivity and provide education, public health, and other amenities for the Malay population. Although these expenditures were large and per capita incomes increased, the per capita incomes of the urban population grew more rapidly. Snodgrass sums up the political impact of this program as follows:

> In political terms, the pre–1969 rural development programme was an exercise in constructive conservatism. By making the life of the rural Malays more comfortable, it hoped to head off both communal and class conflict. But since the programme inevitably contributed to the growth of awareness and ambition in the rural population, and since income inequality was increasing rather than diminishing, the desired contentment and placidity could not be maintained indefinitely.[59]

These and other factors led to the riots of May 13, 1969, which resulted in considerable loss of life and property. The riots not only shook up the Malaysian government but also the Harvard project. One result of the riots was the formation of an authoritarian government, the National Operations Council, under Tun Abdul Razak, which was to rule during the emergency. There was considerable debate in the Harvard group on whether it should work for an authoritarian government and much consultation with Cambridge.

The view for "continuing as usual" was expressed by Just Faaland, then the project director:

> My view is that we should take a position of active cooperation with the Government through the formal and political channels we have, but keep very close, constant watch on political developments, signs of oppression, of repressive social discrimination, etc.[60]

The opposing view was offered by Anders Olgaard, a Danish advisor:

> Tun Razak runs the country. . . ; the "center of power" is near Tun Razak in the EPU. But this is exactly why the Harvard Group

> is bound to be identified with the policy of government, and this is why my suggestion today was — not that we should stay put, even less leave the country — but to cooperate passively rather than actively.[61]

Unfortunately this divergence of views developed into a conflict that created something of a crisis for the project. Faaland espoused strongly the aggressive redistribution measures which came to be known as the New Economic Policy. This alienated him from some of the other advisors, from the leadership of EPU, from certain other officials, and from the Ford Foundation, while allying him closely with certain Malay intellectuals and officials. The crisis lasted until Faaland left the project.

Politically the repercussions of the "emergency" died down in a few months and regular parliamentary government was restored in early 1971 with Tun Razak becoming Prime Minister in the next election. But by that time public policies, including those concerned with development, had changed radically. The New Economic Policy announced by the National Operations Council was to be embodied in the Second Malaysian Five–Year Plan. This policy aimed at an eventual elimination of imbalance among the ethnic groups, not only with respect to income distribution, but also with respect to ownership and control of assets. Specifically, it proposed that by 1990 the difference between Malay and non–Malay per capita incomes should be sharply reduced, the Malay share in employment should be made commensurate with the Malay population, and the Malay stake in the ownership and control of all types of enterprise should be raised to 30 percent. Inevitably this policy would shift the direction of public investment away from an almost exclusive concern with agriculture to the industrial, mining, and commercial sections of the economy.

The Harvard advisors worked with their counterparts on this Second Malaysia Plan, and the Malaysian staff was considerably strengthened by the return from overseas of an able deputy director of the EPU, an Anglo–Indian, C. L. Robless. Indeed the increasing competence of the local staff suggested that the size of the advisory group might well be reduced. When I visisted Kuala Lumpur in February 1972, there were six advisors including Wolfgang Kasper, a German economist, who was assigned to the Bank Negara Malaysia. He informed me that his counterpart was now fully capable of doing the job and I received the same advice from one or two of the advisors in EPU. According to Snodgrass, who had by then been with the project for four years, the caliber of the Malaysian staff had improved steadily. Consequently, in the final three-year renewal of the Ford Foundation grant, the number of advisors was reduced to two, assistance to the economic division of the Treasury was discontinued, and the emphasis was placed on research and training assistance. The project ended in 1975.

Judged by the tests we have proposed, the Malaysia project must be considered a success, although the EPU has declined in importance in recent years. The advisors had been engaged in all the central development issues and policies in Malaysia, and their advice was highly regarded. They left behind an effective planning institution, though it must be said that the performance of the Development Administration Unit was less than outstanding. The training efforts of the project added substantially to the numbers of competent economists in the Malaysia Civil Service. Various members of the successive advisory groups added significantly to the development literature. One indication of the attitude of the Malaysian government towards these efforts was the fact that, after a two-year hiatus, the DAS, which in 1974 had become the Harvard Institute for International Development, was asked to provide advisors for an additional three-year assignment.

Indonesia

The involvement of Harvard advisors in Indonesia has been of longer duration than in Malaysia and more comprehensive than in any other country with the possible exception of Pakistan. Most of these activities have continued under HIID auspices, but three projects belong in the DAS period (1962–1974). The first, begun in 1963 when Sukarno was still president of Indonesia, was advisory to a research agency, the National Economic and Social Research Institute (LEKNAS). This will be considered later, under the heading "Other DAS Projects." The second, starting in 1968, was an advisory service to the newly-established National Development Planning Agency (BAPPENAS). The third, which was an outgrowth of and closely associated with the BAPPENAS activity, was the provision of advisory services to the Directorate of State Investment in the Ministry of Finance. All were financed by the Ford Foundation.

BAPPENAS (the National Development Planning Agency) had been formed shortly after the failed coup of September 30, 1965, when elements of the military, presumably assisted by the Communists, assassinated six generals and attempted to take over power. They were thwarted by General Suharto and his associates and a military government came into being. Although President Sukarno attempted to regain power, he was frustrated and finally deposed in March 1967. Suharto became acting president and later president. There was a strong similarity between these events in Indonesia and the overthrow of Nkrumah in Ghana, which took place in this same period. Sukarno in Indonesia, like Nkrumah in Ghana, had brought into being a country with a strong feeling of nationhood but an economy in shambles. During the period of Sukarno's "Socialism à la Indonesia" (1958–1966) per capita incomes declined, foreign–exchange earnings fell by a third, and inflation became rampant. Foreign reserves declined from $313 million in 1960 to $17 million in March 1967.

The responsibility of restoring order to the economy was assigned to the Sultan of Jogjakarta and he brought into the government five economists, three of whom were PhDs from Berkeley. They formed the nucleus of the "Berkeley Mafia," products of the Ford Foundation–financed affiliation between University of California at Berkeley and the University of Indonesia. This team was responsible for designing a stabilization program in collaboration with the IMF, implemented in October 1966. Immediately after adoption of the program the team invited a DAS advisor, David Cole, to visit Indonesia and consult on further measures to assure effective stabilization and lay the foundation for recovery. The leader of the team was Professor Widjojo Nitisastro, who became a member of the cabinet and head of BAPPENAS in 1967. He and his technical colleagues in other ministries saw the task as falling in three stages: stabilization, rehabilitation, and development.[62] The task was a difficult one. In Benjamin Higgins's 1968 assessment, "Indonesia must surely be accounted the number one failure among the major underdeveloped countries."[63]

Nevertheless, by the time the first DAS team came on the scene, July 1, 1968, inflation was coming under control, and a five–year development plan (Repelita I) was in preparation. The first task of the advisors was to assist in the completion of this plan which, before the end of the year, had been accepted by the President and the cabinet. It was, however, a limited one which, because of data limitations, lacked a macroeconomic framework:

> Instead it is a pulling together of partial sectoral rehabilitation and expansion programs which are balanced against political and foreign–financed resources.[64]

One of the initial policy areas in which the DAS advisors played a significant role was the interest rate reform of September 1968 which helped to stabilize the exchange rate, increase foreign–exchange reserves, and gave the banking system non–inflationary loanable funds.

The acting director, later director of the DAS project, was William Hollinger, who succeeded Richard Gilbert. Hollinger, the former director of the DAS project in Liberia, had had earlier experience in Indonesia. The initial contract was renewed three times providing for four or five advisors (three in the last stage) and a varying number of consultants. The Ford Foundation financing of the team ended in 1976, though a few individuals continued to work with BAPPENAS after this date. It is this eight years of experience from 1968 to 1976 that is under discussion here. Altogether, the Foundation spent $2,502,200 on the BAPPENAS venture.

Indonesia did not lack foreign advisors. Both the International Monetary Fund and the International Bank for Research and Development (World Bank) had permanent teams in Jakarta. And there were Dutch, Japanese, and Australian advisors, not to mention the involvement of the Asian Development Bank and various bilateral aid missions. There was some fear that the DAS mission would work at cross–purposes with other advisors to BAPPENAS. But, according to Hollinger, this did not happen and a natural division of labor emerged:

> The DAS concentrates on broad policy; the IBRD team on sector programs and project development; the Tinbergen team (from Holland) on three specific subject matters—regional planning, manpower, and aid management; the Okita project (Japan) has one man physically present but substantively invisible.[65]

Hollinger goes on to say relations with the IMF "have not been as bad as might have feared, nor nearly so good or smooth as those with, say, the IBRD."

The World Bank Mission was, at this stage, headed by Bernard Bell, who was clearly the most effective foreign advisor to the Indonesian government. He and his team worked closely with the DAS. According to a Harvard Advisory Group report, BAPPENAS had two principal functions:

> (a) The planning process proper: . . . preparation of the annual development budget; and the establishment of implementaton procedures for the plan.
>
> (b) Activities in economic areas which are BAPPENAS' responsibility by reason of its charter and *ad hoc* assignments from the President. These include management of project negotiations, credit policies and programs, rice price policy, and general staff work for government.[66]

Apart from its chairman and three or four senior officials, BAPPENAS was a weak organization in 1968. This was true of the Indonesian civil service in general—a thin layer of competence at the top administering a relatively untrained and undermotivated staff, far weaker than the civil services of India or Pakistan. In part this was the result of very low salary scales, which forced all who could find extra jobs to do so; in part it was the product of a weak educational structure and Dutch exclusion of Indonesians from both education and the bureaucracy. On the other hand,

> The adverse affects on the DAS team [of limited counterparts within BAPPENAS] are substantially offset by the opportunity, strongly encouraged by the Chairman, to work also with such related agencies as the Ministries of Finance and Trade and the Central Bank.[67]

In addition to these agencies the advisors worked closely with the Ministry of Industries and with Bulog, the agency charged with the marketing and pricing of rice. The Harvard Group gave a good deal of attention to training, holding seminars in BAPPENAS and participating in teaching economic courses in the University. Lester Gordon, then Director of DAS, and J. Price Gittinger of the World Bank undertook, in the spring of 1971, a special study of BAPPENAS staff development and needs, the recommendations of which were accepted and partially put into effect.

Strengthening the planning and project preparation process got underway shortly after the acceptance of the first plan and, in the light of serious deficiencies in relevant information, sizable groups of consultants were brought to Indonesia in the summers of 1969, 1970, and 1971 from Britain, Japan, Germany, Holland, and the United States. Although this effort was financed by bilateral aid programs, the coordination of these studies was assisted by the Harvard advisory group. The outline and statement of principles of the Second Plan was completed in October 1972. The year before that in the general elections, Golkar, the government's political organization, won 62.8 percent of the vote and was assured of overwhelming support in Parliament until 1978. Indonesia had by this time acquired that most necessary condition of a successful development effort—a government deeply concerned with development and able to put politically difficult policies into effect. It was not a government devoid of corruption—indeed corruption was endemic—but this did not prevent a real growth rate of 6 to 7 percent a year.

It is impossible in this space to assess the principal policy recommendations of the Harvard group, but one which was put into effect deserves mention. This was the district level (Kabupaten) public works program initiated in 1970. Y. B. de Witt, known as "Jan Tinbergen's man" in Indonesia, and Richard Patten of the DAS seem to have been the idea men behind this program. Patten had been previously engaged in the public works program in East Pakistan. The Kabupaten program was financed by the central government, using, in part, PL 480 imports. The public works to be constructed included local market buildings, roads, irrigation projects, etc., which were chosen, within specified limits, by district governments. The engineering was done at a sub–provincial level and supervised by provincial governments. Work was assigned to local contractors in competitive bidding and workers were paid the prevailing wage for unskilled labor. In 1971, 3.5 million workers were employed at an average of 100 days for the year. In addition to its public works and employment effects, it was a program of considerable political significance and strongly supported by the president.

Gustav Papanek became director of the project in 1972 and was followed by Malcolm Gillis in 1973. Gillis had by that time spent a considerable period in Indonesia, serving as advisor to the Minister of Finance. The Indonesian government carried through a successful devaluation in August 1971 and, on April 1, 1974, the Second Five–Year Plan (Repelita II) went into effect. By that time, BAPPENAS had moved from coping with crises to dealing with longer–term structural and institutional changes in the economy. Reporting in June 1972, Papanek noted that "Compared to, say, two years earlier, the planning agency is incomparably stronger in terms of staff." New people had returned from abroad. He noted, though, that the junior staff remained inadequate.[68]

During the last two years of the project, the director was Clive Gray, who had previously directed the DAS planning assistance in Ethiopia and, before that, had been a member of the Colombia team. There were now only three advisors plus six consultants. Major attention was paid to training, with seminars and courses, not only in BAPPENAS, but in the university and in the Ministry of Transport. A member of the team designed a program to combat soil erosion in Java, involving the cooperation of local communities, which was incorporated in the government budget for 1977. A good deal of work was done on tax reform with the assistance of three consultants from Harvard: Richard and Peggy Musgrave from the economics department and Stanley Surrey from the Law School. The resident advisory project terminated July 1, 1976.

On the whole the BAPPENAS project must be judged to have been a successful one. Working not only with BAPPENAS but with all the principal economic agencies of government, the advisors made a significant contribution to economic policy. And BAPPENAS was a much stronger agency in 1976 than it had been in 1968, in large part because of the training efforts of the Harvard group and the World Bank. Although individual planning advisors recruited by Harvard continued to be employed after 1976, it was no longer felt that a team was necessary. The fact that the Indonesian government has continued to rely on the Harvard Institute for International Development for technical assistance in a wide range of activities gives some indication that the BAPPENAS effort was valued. Moreover, a substantial number of publications on the Indonesian economy has resulted from these activities.

The other Indonesian project belonging to the DAS period began when Ali Wardhana, Minister of Finance, in a letter of July 22, 1971, to the Ford Foundation representative in Indonesia, asked for financial help to support a mission to advise on the management of public–sector enterprises. Professor Paul McAvoy, then of the MIT faculty, had already paid a visit to Indonesia and the grant to DAS was to cover his continuing work and that of two assistants. There were some 140 state enterprises in industry, agriculture, transport, and trade, previously under the custodial responsibility of various ministers and it was proposed to transfer responsibility for the government equity to the newly–formed Directorate of State Enterprises in the Ministry of Finance. These enterprises were to be converted into limited liability companies (perseros) in which the government owned all the equity. According to Ali Wardhana, "Some are well managed and are producing revenue for the state; others are poorly managed and have been a burden on the state's resources." In fact, almost all of them were loss-makers and constituted a severe drain on the budget.

It was intended that many, if not most, of these companies would be sold to private investors and the main objective of the advisory project was to provide tests of performance that would be useful to potential investors and to the Directorate of State Enterprises. Although many useful papers were written, few if any companies were sold off and, a few years later, custodial responsibility was retransferred from the Ministry of Finance to the operating ministries. Losses by state-owned enterprises continue to plague the Indonesian government.

Ethiopia

The last DAS advisory group to a planning commission worked in Ethiopia from 1971 to 1975. It was financed by the U.N. Development Programme and the Imperial Government with the World Bank serving as the executing agency. Harvard's interest in Ethopia was stimulated by Ato Belai Abbai, head of the newly–formed Planning Commission Office and a former Public Service Fellow at Harvard. At his invitation, Gustav Papenek visited Addis Ababa early in 1970. He was impressed both by the low level of development and the rapid rate of change:

> It is possible that the Planning Commission will turn out to be an ineffective agency. . . our project (if any) might come to an inglorious end. On the other hand, the government seems to realize that it badly needs technocrats, they have been increasingly influential, and the rapid change in the society is probably irreversible, so there is a real possibility of a highly interesting and highly useful advisory project.[69]

The UNDP sent a mission in April 1970 to evaluate the request of the Government of Ethiopia for assistance in development planning. The mission reported that "after years of external assistance from different sources, the Ethiopian staff of the Planning Commission remains essentially weak."[70] They recommended a three–year program with 28 man–years of advisors, one man–year of consultants, and 14 man–years of fellowships. The project was to begin January 1, 1971, but two advisors arrived to begin preliminary work in August 1970.

Ethiopia was, with the possible exception of Liberia, the least developed economy the DAS had encountered. The population of 25 million generated a national income estimated at $2 billion, yielding a per capita income of $50 to $60. It was a distinctly feudal society with His Imperial Majesty supported by a land–holding aristocracy and a powerful land–rich church. In the 1950s only 2 percent of the primary school age cohort was in school. A college was founded in the 1950s and Haile Selassie I University was established in the 1960s. But large numbers of young Ethiopians were being sent abroad for training and the number of semi–educated technocrats was increasing rapidly.

The first project director was Clive Gray, already mentioned in connection with Colombia and Indonesia. When the full complement of nine advisors was assembled, six were employed in the Planning Commission Office, and one each in the Central Statistical Office, the Ministry of Education, and the Ministry of Communications, Transport and Posts. More than in most DAS projects, the work of the advisors was concerned with training and data collection. In his first report, the director indicated that highest priority had been given to the selection of people for overseas training. During the course of the project, 72 Ethiopians were sent abroad.

Courses in national accounts were given at the Planning Commission Office and regular seminars on economic development were held for government officials both from that office and from other agencies. Lectures on economics were given by advisors at the university. An industrial census was prepared, new measures of unemployment were devised, the national accounts overhauled, and educational statistics improved.

A DAS Report indicates that the regular work load included:

> Preparing the annual development budget, processing agency requests for budget allocations, evaluating projects, and monitoring the implementation of the Third Five–Year Development Plan (originally scheduled to end in July 1973 but extended for an additional year in the light of difficult economic circumstances in the Plan's first two years).[71]

A major reshuffle of the Council of Ministers occurred in August 1971 when Abbai was elevated to the Council of Ministers as Minister of Land Reform and Administration. His place as head of the Planning Commission Office was taken by Ato Tekalign Gedamu, an economist who had served most recently as general manager of the Development Bank of Ethiopia and had been a Public Service Fellow at Harvard in 1965–66. Disturbances at the university, which included several deaths, abolition of the Student Union, and mass expulsion, gave an indication of political difficulties to come. When I visited Addis Ababa in February 1972, I had the impression that the advisors were really being used as staff by the head of the planning office rather than as advisors to their counterparts.

Clive Gray left as head of the project in October 1972 to join the project in Indonesia and his place was taken by Lars Kalderen, head of the Bilateral Aid Department in the Swedish Ministry of Foreign Affairs. During the next year and a half, the advisors were mainly concerned with working with the planning office and the various economic ministries on the Fourth Five–Year Plan, an outline of which was accepted by the Council of Ministers. Improvement in the caliber of the Ethiopian staff permitted a closer collaboration with counterparts.

The contract with the Imperial Government of Ethiopia and the UNDP was renewed late in 1973, but political disturbances beginning in February 1974 developed into a bloody overthrow of the government of Emperor Haile Selassie and its replacement by a military regime. As a result, the DAS personnel were not replaced when their contracts expired and by the end of 1974 the number of advisors was down to three. In May

1975 it was agreed among the contracting parties to end all activities on August 15 of that year.

What would have been accomplished by the DAS project in Ethiopia if it had continued is unclear. The Planning Commission Office had been considerably strengthened, the statistical basis for planning had been substantially improved, and the economic policymaking agencies of the government brought into more effective cooperation. But all or most of this was lost in the revolution, and a number of the senior officials with whom the Harvard group had worked were either imprisoned or driven into exile.

Other DAS Projects

Early in its existence the DAS undertook two small advisory projects to overseas research organizations. One was in Indonesia and the other in Argentina; neither was very productive.

In Indonesia, the Ford Foundation in March 1963 financed a small (DAS) advisory mission to the National Economic and Social Research Institute (Leknas). The first resident advisors under a DAS contract were Professor Donald J. Blake, formerly of the faculty of the University of Indonesia, and Professor Everett Hawkins of the University of Wisconsin. During this early period Nathan Keyfitz, then of the University of Chicago, served as a consultant on demographic problems. A later, long–term advisor was Kurt Martin of the University of Manchester, who had previously been a member of the Iran project. Leknas was initially a refuge for the returning Berkeley/Ford–trained economists. It served as the home for the economics team from 1963 until 1967, when it was drawn into the government. Professor Widjojo was the first director and Ali Wardana the Deputy Director of Leknas.

The role of the advisors was primarily to assist in the framing of research programs on economic and social aspects of development and secondarily to help select promising Indonesians for foreign training. The second function was probably more effectively performed than the first. When the original members of the Indonesian staff were drawn into government employment in 1967–68, the Institute became a rather tenuous enterprise which never bloomed as an effective research organization. The DAS continued to supply advisors and consultants until December 31, 1972, when the project ended.

The project in Argentina was even less successful. The Di Tella Institute was a private research organization established by Torcuate di Tella, one of Argentina's wealthy and philanthropic businessmen. It also received support from the Ford Foundation. The director of the Institute was Guillermo Edelberg, a former student of the Harvard Business School. The staff included about 20 Argentinians who were getting their degrees abroad and were mainly engaged in writing their dissertations. But the Institute was also engaged in contract research for various departments of government. A Ford Foundation grant in 1963 provided a DAS advisor and a number of consultants, but effective relations between the advisory group and the Argentine staff never developed. According to the Center for International Affairs Report for 1965–66, "In Argentina the DAS relationship with Di Tella Institute produced few benefits for either party. . . . It was agreed to let the arrangement expire as of June 30, 1966."[72]

In the closing years of the DAS period three new projects were undertaken which were carried on mainly under HIID auspices. They were in Tanzania, Korea, and Nicaragua.

The DAS had long wished for an involvement in Tanzania and an opportunity appeared to develop at a conference in Sussex early in 1970. According to a memo from Lester Gordon to the DAS Advisory Committee on June 1, 1970:

> Beginning with very tentative inquiries then, in which it was clear that the government had doubts about involvement with a "group" of foreigners, an American–based institution and individuals who might not be sympathetic with the nation's socialist orientation, we have been asked to assist in the development of a long–term industrial strategy. The request for such limited support apparently reflects a wish to try us out and to keep our numbers small and our scope limited.

After several visits from DAS personnel to Dar es Salaam, the Tanzanian government sought and found financing from the UNDP for a three–year, three–man project. The executing agency was the United Nations Industrial Development Organization (UNIDO). The three advisors, arriving early in 1972, were Michael Roemer, project director; Gene Tidrick, trade specialist; and David Williams, industry studies. The advisors were located in the Ministry of Economic Affairs and Development Planning. In mid–1974, Roemer returned to Cambridge, David Williams took over as project director, and Robert Rice, of the University of Hawaii, joined the staff.

The DAS Final Report, covering 1972 to 1974, contains a detailed account of the work of the advisors during the first two years of the Tanzanian project.[73] In collaboration with their counterparts, the Harvard term undertook studies of 29 industries, including projections of output and employment under alternative strategies. These studies were reviewed by a governmental "industry working party" which made recommendations concerning an industrial strategy to be incorporated in Tanzania's Third Five–Year Plan. During the third year of the project the advisors were concerned with plan implementation, with the preparation of a project evaluation manual, and with the teaching of a number of courses and seminars attended by officials from development agencies and students from the University of Dar es Salaam.[74] The Tanzania project was particularly noteworthy for its careful examination of the alternative industrial strategies available to a country at an early stage of development.

The most extensive and the most successful research advisory project undertaken by the DAS began in South Korea in 1972, financed by USAID and the Korean government. The project, directed by David Cole, provided advisors and consultants to the Korea Development Institute (KDI) which was organized in 1971 to undertake research on development policy. The staff of KDI was mainly composed of recent PhDs from American universities. The director was Kim Mahn Je, a close advisor to government. In mid–1972 three economists from Harvard, Robert Dorfman, Simon Kuznets, and Dwight Perkins, participated in a symposium at KDI concerned with the organization of policy research. One long–term resident researcher, Leroy Jones, and a series of short–term consultants served as advisors on the early research projects conducted by KDI staff members. The DAS also organized overseas training in the U.S. for 27 junior staff from the KDI. The KDI developed into a competent and highly regarded research organization, the principal research arm of the Korean Economic Planning Board. Later it undertook, jointly with HIID, an extensive study of the economic and social modernization of Korea.[75] The formal HIID relationship with KDI ended in 1980.

In Nicaragua, following the devastating earthquake in Managua in 1972, the DAS undertook a contract with the Central American Institute of Business Administration (INCAE). The first assignment was planning the reconstruction of the devastated area. But the main task was working with INCAE to develop a capacity to assist Central American development institutions and also to assist enterprises both public and private. The first contract, from May 1973 to December 1974, was mainly financed by an AID loan to the Nicaraguan government and provided for 3 man–years of resident advisors and one man–year of consultants. The first project director was Olaf Saetersdal of the Ministry of Finance in Norway. When the project was extended in 1975, Richard Mallon of the HIID staff and Robert Salomon, Senior Economist of the Organization of American States, became resident advisors.

By the time the project had ended in November 1977, INCAE was mounting a number of training programs attended by participants from all the Central American countries and had entered into advisory contracts with public and private enterprises in Nicaragua, Costa Rica, Honduras, El Salvador, and Guatemala.

Two Aborted Projects

A three–man mission, financed by the U.N. Development Programme, visited Peru between July and September 1971 to consider a proposal to assist the National Planning Institute (INP) establish an applied socio–economic research center. A follow–up visit was made in January 1972, and in the summer of that year Richard Mallon spent seven weeks and Lance Taylor one week in Lima. A proposal was prepared for 8 man–years of advisory service and 8–12 months of consultants between 1972 to 1974, to cost $440,000, which would be financed by the UNDP. But "it proved impossible to reach a mutually satisfactory agreement between the UNDP, the INP and the DAS on a longer term contract" and the project came to an end September 1972.[76] In fact, it was the advice of the Economic Commission for Latin America (ECLA) to the Peruvian Government that killed the project. ECLA pushed hard for the inclusion of contract clauses inconsistent with Harvard's concept of academic freedom.

Another aborted project was to have been performed within the United States. In 1970 the possibility emerged of a joint DAS–Kennedy Institute project to assist the Delta Foundation of Greenville, Mississippi, to improve the productivity of farmers and to explore the potential of black entrepreneurship in commercial and industrial undertakings in the Mississippi Delta. It was thought that the experience of the DAS in similar overseas activities would be relevant.[77]

The Delta Foundation represented most of the civil rights leadership and black activist groups on the Mississippi Delta and had been supported by small grants from the Ford Foundation. The Delta Foundation had an interest in tapping the resources of the Cambridge intellectual community and believed that an association with the DAS would generate more resources from the Ford Foundation.

After some 18 months of discussion a DAS mission of Walter Falcon, Carl Gotsch, and Robert Aulston visited Greenville to work out a proposal which called for a grant of $270,000 over a three–year period.[78] The Ford Foundation, however, was not interested and the project was abandoned.

DAS, Harvard University, and the Ford Foundation

In 1969, after the DAS had been in operation for seven years, the president of Harvard appointed a committee to look into the relations between the Development Advisory Service and the University. Robert Dorfman was the chairman. The charge to the committee was to consider "whether the DAS was making a large enough contribution to Harvard to justify continuing it as a university activity, whether the current administrative arrangements were appropriate and effective, and whether any changes in organization and function would be advantageous." Preliminary discussions disclosed that one area of concern both to members of the DAS and to others in the University was the comparative remoteness of the DAS from the other activities of the University.[79]

The DAS at that stage was already a sizable organization with a budget, in 1967–68, of about $3 million. Of this the Ford Foundation contribution was $1.2 million; the UNDP, $750,000; client countries, $650,000; AID, $150,000 (all for research or fellowships); and Harvard, $22,000 (all for DAS teaching).

The University's financial contribution was negligible. But this was not true of the contribution of faculty time. Although there were no tenured members of the faculty engaged full time either in Cambridge or overseas, Raymond Vernon had served half time for three years as Director, the members of the Advisory Committee had given time to the enterprise, and a significant number of faculty members, including Chenery, Leontief, Kuznets, Dorfman, Vernon, Mason, Fainsod, Musgrave, and others, had served abroad as consultants. In addition some 15 to 20 younger members of University departments, principally economists, had served as consultants or were engaged in Cambridge-based research on development problems.

The question was what did the University get, if anything, out of this activity? One issue involved in answering this question was whether a university should consider it a useful, if not necessary, function to provide technical assistance to less–advantaged areas or countries. According to the Dorfman Report, "The professional reputation of the DAS in the performance of these tasks is uniquely high," though how much credit accrued to the University on this account was not made clear. If this prestige factor was ignored, the potential contribution of the DAS to Harvard was in teaching and research. Neither of these activities was very highly developed in the early years of the DAS.

According to the Dorfman Report, "No member of the DAS has a regular teaching appointment in the university." Though it was true that no member of the core staff had a formal teaching assignment, the staff participated in a number of courses and seminars for which the DAS received compensation. This accounted for the $22,000 the university contributed in 1967–68. Furthermore, both tenured and non–tenured members of the faculty who had served as consultants abroad in DAS projects, brought this experience into teaching.

"The major shortcoming of the DAS, regarded as a university function," according to the report, "has been in the field of research . . . There is no formalized program for integrating and collating the varied experience of the advisors or of the different countries in which they have served." The report noted that six books and over 50 pamphlets and articles had been published by people connected with the DAS in addition to over 100 multilithed papers and reports. This may have been inadequate but was hardly derisory. Still "there was no large–scale research effort on the development process."

Whatever deficiencies existed in the research effort were in part being rectified. A director of research, Walter Falcon, had been appointed in 1966, and sizable grants for research were being received from AID. The DAS was also cooperating closely with the Project for Quantitative Research in Economic Development in the Center for International Affairs and with the Transport Research Project in the Department of Economics. After a somewhat slow start research activities were increasing rapidly.

Still, as the Dorfman Report pointed out, the DAS was rather remote from the University. "The general feeling of the members of the DAS is that they are guests of the university rather than full–fledged members." And it was with this in mind that the committee made its major recommendations.

1) Two persons should be added at the senior level whose obligations for teaching and research should not be secondary to their involvement in advisory work. (They should probably be in the John F. Kennedy School of Government.)

2) The Director of the DAS should be a tenured member of the Kennedy School of Government or some department of the University.

3) Younger men or women—Ph.D. candidates or recent PhDs—should be added to the research staff and paid for from overseas contracts.

4) In all future contracts and contract renewals, the DAS should make very strong efforts to assure that a reasonable part of the budget be earmarked for research and training purposes.

There was no suggestion in the report that Harvard pay for any of this. And it is doubtful whether the committee realized how difficult it would be to convince countries that some part of the resources available for advisory services to their government should be used for general research on development based in Cambridge. There was one other difficulty that would always plague the DAS and other unconventional appendages of the university. If a new appointment were left to a department or school, would proper attention be paid to the qualification of a candidate as an overseas advisor? These qualities are not necessarily the same as those of a first rate scholar or teacher. I am fairly confident that if the economics department had been given two tenure appointments, half of whose time was to be allocated to the DAS, the candidates would be considered only on the basis of their qualifications as technical economists. Whether the Kennedy School of Government would consider qualifications so narrowly is difficult to say.

In any case the DAS, acting on a generous interpretation of the Dorfman Committee's recommendation, asked the Ford Foundation to finance four tenure appointments, half of whose time would be devoted to the Service. To consider this request and, in addition, to evaluate the activities of an institution with which the Foundation had been so closely engaged, the Foundation appointed a committee which reported in March 1971.[80] By that time the DAS had been in existence for almost ten years. As of July 1, 1970, the cumulative project costs of the DAS had been $13 million, of which the Foundation had contributed $6 million.

The Foundation's committee, in its investigation, "hoped to learn more about the benefits and costs *to a university* of associating an advisory service closely with its more traditional scholarly activities," "*to a developing country* of using DAS," and "*to the Foundation* in supporting DAS as compared with alternative ways of achieving similar results."

With respect to the University, the Foundation's committee considered the contribution to teaching to be "substantial," and the contribution to research, "potentially important." Prior to 1966–67, research by DAS personnel had been financed largely out of project costs. "Since that time," the committee noted, "USAID has financed additional research by the DAS in amounts which had accumulated to $632,000 by July 1, 1970, and which were running at the annual rate of $200,000 in 1969–70." Moreover, as a result of the Dorfman Report, the research activities of the DAS had been substantially revamped in 1969–70 to form a single development research group (a committee of which undertook a review of all research proposals) and to focus the research program on a few priority issues.

The Ford Foundation's committee, however, cautioned that:

> Sponsoring the DAS does entail risks as well as benefits to the university, and these risks lie at the heart of the discussions on the propriety of extending the university's mantle over DAS activities. Operating as it often does at the highest level of policy, the association of the DAS with certain governments abroad appears to some observers to be inconsistent with the objectives of a university. Research may be limited and conditioned by these associations, and indeed may become partisan rather than objective . . .
>
> Many at Harvard also worry about the implicit conflict of interest between the confidential nature of advisory activities and the free flow of information and ideas that is crucial to objective research . . .
>
> We do not wish to romanticize the objectivity of the normal run of scholarly research, but we do feel that there has been and will continue to be some inherent conflict between the research and advisory functions of the DAS. It is to the credit of the DAS and to Harvard University that these issues are openly exposed and widely discussed.

This is indeed an issue, but in practice it is perhaps not as significant as the report to the Ford Foundation suggests. DAS and HIID, its successor, have made it clear to governments that Harvard University does not prohibit publication of any kind and will not sign any contract that asks it to do so. HIID asks each advisor who wishes to publish to show the host institution or government what is to be published and to give them the opportunity to suggest changes and ask for deletions. If such suggested changes or deletions deal with sensitive data or information, the advisor is asked to acquiesce. In thirty years of experience there have been only one or two instances in which governments have objected to what was published.

In fact, governments have been much more willing to accept these conditions than has the United Nations, which has given DAS and HIID considerable difficulty. The U.N., as a matter of form, includes in all its contracts a statement that the institution supplying the advisor, e.g. Harvard University, will ensure that its employees do not publish information obtained through the project without prior clearance. This nearly caused negotiations on the Tanzania contract to collapse, and it was only after long negotiations with Harvard lawyers that compromise language was reached. The same issue arose in negotiations with the U.N. over projects in Malaysia and Sri Lanka. In both cases it was explained to the government why the University could not sign the suggested U.N. contract and in both cases the governments informed the U.N. that they were satisfied to have offending clauses deleted.

In Peru, as indicated elsewhere, a promising project was aborted because of U.N. insistence on clauses that Harvard could not accept. This difficulty is undoubtedly more significant in connection with the advisory projects to planning commissions, where the advisors were concerned with central issues of development policy, than with advice to research organizations or with the more technical advisory assignments on sectoral and managerial issues with which HIID has been primarily concerned. Contact with central policy issues certainly yields a greater understanding of the development process than is vouchsafed to outsiders, but it also carries with it limitations on what can be revealed. Constraining publication is inimical to objective research if it leads to partisan support of government policies with which the advisor has been connected. There may have been a few examples of DAS research in which this has been the case but, if so, they are unknown to me. The committee appointed by the Ford Foundation did not express an opinion on whether the benefits of access to sensitive information is outweighed by loss of objectivity, but was correct in raising the issue.

The usefulness of the DAS to the less developed countries which have been advised depends upon: (1) the quality of the advice and of the advisors, and (2) the contribution to training and institution building. The Foundation's committee was inclined to give the DAS higher marks on the former activity than on the latter. It should be noted that host countries have usually emphasized the importance of the first activity. With respect to this the Ford Foundation committee reported:

> The less developed countries have found particularly valuable the continuing university link which is a unique feature of the DAS. The quality of advisors for the overseas projects of the DAS has been remarkably high compared with similar technical assistance missions; the Harvard name implies excellence; and the University mantle protects the independence and the integrity of the advisor much more effectively than employment of most donor agencies or host institutions could do. They also expect advisors to identify more closely with indigenous needs and aspirations, reducing concerns about divided loyalties, ideological overtones and influence by foreign governments.

On the other hand, as the committee observed, this is a "second best solution" as compared with competent local staff. The development of competence may require primary attention to training and institution building, which brings us to the considerations other than advisory with which the DAS should be concerned. On this the committee spoke as follows:

> Probably the most critical comments we have received about the DAS relate to its activities in developing indigenous planning skills. . .
>
> The essential components of a staff development program are (1) local teaching programs, (2) education and training abroad, and (3) counterpart training. Too often DAS teams have emphasized the second component and have neglected both the first and the third. The comprehensive effort now being made in Indonesia is an exception.

This is probably a valid criticism, though, as noted above, DAS teams were usually under severe pressure by host governments to maximize their advisory activities at the expense of training and institution building.

The fact of the matter is that the DAS undertook to serve a number of clients not all of whose interests were identical. The University was primarily interested in contributions to teaching and research. The financing agencies—certainly the Ford Foundation—were primarily interested in training and institution building. The host governments were primarily interested in advisory services and, to a lesser extent, in training and institution building. Balancing these diverse interests was not always an easy task. As the Ford Foundation's committee observed, "These differences have imposed strains on the DAS, and its management has been continuously occupied, with mixed results, to find weights which would be acceptable to other parties, and satisfactory to itself."

Finally, the committee considered the value of DAS services to its financial supporters, particularly the Ford Foundation, as compared with alternative ways of providing similar services. It concluded that the use of private consulting firms would have been more expensive and the research and teaching opportunities negligible. The committee asked the Foundation to calculate the cost of direct hire to the Foundation and compare it against using the DAS. "The principal conclusion was that while the full per man year cost of the DAS was slightly higher than the Ford Foundation direct hire, the difference was not significant, particularly if account is taken of differences in teaching and research benefits."

On the whole the committee concluded:

> The value of the DAS to its sources of financial support and to other international agencies concerned with providing foreign aid and technical assistance has been considerable. Its field teams have introduced elements of creativity, rationality and analysis into development planning and project evaluation that have improved substantially the basis of aid decisions. Moreover the university setting of the DAS has enabled it to perform its administrative, recruiting and backstopping responsibilities in ways that donors could not easily duplicate.

This report to the Ford Foundation was not too well received by the DAS, largely because it recommended against the financing of four additional positions at Harvard. But the report provided by far the most careful and discriminating evaluation of the institution thus far undertaken.

Some Final Remarks on the DAS

As the DAS moved into its twelfth year, 1973–74, there were still reservations in the University concerning its appropriate role. It was almost exclusively staffed by economists, though development clearly involved things other than economics. Shouldn't other disciplines such as political science, anthropology, management, etc., be represented? No tenured member of the faculty was on the staff of the DAS. Should not at least the Director be such a member? The core staff positions of the DAS were difficult to fill. A number of the ten authorized positions had not been filled and the DAS had been turned down in certain of its efforts to recruit senior staff. This was not entirely a matter of money. Despite contributions to teaching and research by DAS staff, its members continued to be regarded, by themselves and others, as not quite full–fledged members of the University. Finally, the requests for advisory assistance to planning commissions which had been the bread and butter of DAS activities were clearly on the decline. Did the DAS have a future and, if so, in what areas? For these and other reasons, there was active discussion which led in 1974 to the formation of the Harvard Institute for International Development (HIID) to replace the Development Advisory Service (DAS).

3. The Third Stage: The Harvard Institute for International Development

The Harvard Institute for International Development was proposed by a faculty committee which was appointed by President Bok of Harvard and which reported to the President and Fellows of Harvard College on July 19, 1973.[81] The two major considerations guiding the committee's deliberations were: (1) the need to broaden the scope of advising, teaching and research activities to include disciplines other than economics and thus to involve faculties of the University other than the economics department; and (2) the need to incorporate the performance of international activities more closely into the work of the University, both institutionally and functionally.

After considerable discussion and debate the President and Fellows (the Harvard Corporation) accepted the main recommendations of the committee and HIID came into existence in 1974 under the direction of Lester Gordon. Initially the department of economics, the School of Public Health, and the Graduate School of Education participated actively, but other departments and schools of the University were encouraged to participate if and when their overseas activities could be effectively managed by HIID. Subsequently the departments of anthropology and sociology played an active role.

HIID reports to the president of the University through a Committee of Deans chaired by the Dean of the Faculty of Arts and Sciences. Initially the other members of the Committee of Deans were drawn from the School of Public Health, the Graduate School of Education, and the Graduate School of Design. Later, in 1980, the deans of the Kennedy School of Government and the Graduate School of Business Administration were added. Provision was made for a Faculty Council to represent all departments and schools of the University interested in overseas development. The Council "shall consider all matters requiring or likely to require the action or attention of the President and Corporation; maintain a continuing review of the activities of the Institute; and make recommendations on such matters to the Subcommittee of Deans and the Director of the Institute."[82] Questions of corporation appointments, contract negotiations, supervision of the effectiveness of Institute activity, and financial plans and performance came under the purview of the Committee of Deans. The Faculty Council was chaired by Professor Raymond Vernon of the Graduate School of Business Administration and later Clarence Dillon Professor of International Affairs, and he served until his retirement in 1984.

The "Constitution" of HIID, approved by the President and Fellows, provided for a number of professional categories. Modeled on the DAS advisors, a core group of Institute Fellows was appointed whose tenure was "without limit of time." This meant essentially that if HIID were to be discontinued, Institute Fellows would be guaranteed 18 months at Harvard to find other jobs. A $500,000 grant from the Ford Foundation to the DAS was available for this purpose and the University pledged additional funds if necessary. In fact the initial grant from the Foundation was apparently more than adequate for this purpose. Of the seven Development Advisors and one Institute Fellow who left the organization between 1962 and 1984, one retired and seven moved to other jobs. Institute Fellows are expected to spend at least half their time abroad either as directors of projects or frequent visitors to overseas projects. While in Cambridge they are engaged in teaching, research, and the backstopping of overseas projects. In fact, all the Institute Fellows have teaching appointments in various departments and schools. When HIID was founded in 1974, seven Development Advisors, all economists, were appointed to the position of Institute Fellows. Shortly afterwards, Institute Fellows were appointed in public health, education, and sociology. As of May 1984, there were nine Institute Fellows, in addition to the Director and Executive Director of HIID.

A second professional category was comprised of Faculty Fellows, whose primary appointments were as teaching faculty of the University. Their connections with HIID were on a part–time basis and for a specific period of time. The intention was—and the effect has been—to bring HIID in closer contact with the University. There have been six Faculty Fellows, Professors Hollis Chenery and Dwight Perkins of the department of economics, Russell Davis of the Graduate School of Education, Peter Timmer of the Graduate School of Business Administration, Brian Berry of the Graduate School of Design, and Dieter Koch–Weser of the School of Medicine.

Other professional categories included Fellows of the Institute, Institute Associates, Research Associates, Visiting Scholars, Project Associates (outside professionals recruited to work on overseas projects), supported by administrative and management staff. As of June 1986, HIID employed some 84 professionals, over 30 of whom were overseas.

HIID was established in a period of declining interest—within the United States and, to some extent, elsewhere—in the fate of the less developed world. Indeed there were those who predicted a short life and not a merry one. As the Director, Lester Gordon, wrote in 1980, in his final report:

> America's interest in the developing world was at a low ebb. Governmental assistance programs and those of private foundations had reached a nadir or were heading downward. Sources of finance for HIID's projected service activities abroad were contracting as it was opening its door. Funding for development research was also declining and narrowing in scope. Despite strong support in many other ways, the university was unable to step into the breach without violating its own rule that each tub must float on its own financial bottom. Further there were signs that some developing nations felt less need of the traditional brands of technical assistance. Their own stock of trained professionals had grown and pride in their national self–sufficiency was increasingly evident.[83]

Indeed there were a few years during the DAS period and early in the history of HIID when the organization ran at a loss and had to borrow from the University. These arrears were not cleared up until 1982. Early in the 1970s the Ford Foundation ceased to regard the institution as a preferred agent in the promotion of its overseas development interests and although the Foundation has made small grants to HIID, mainly for training projects, it has been a minor source of funding since 1974. Furthermore, the demand from developing countries for assistance to planning commissions, which had been the principal activity of the DAS, dried up. New types of projects and new sources of financing had to be found.

When HIID was formed it inherited seven overseas projects from the DAS. By the end of the second year four projects were terminated according to plan and one (Ethiopia) because of a revolution. During the same period six new overseas projects were initiated and their character and financing indicate the changes that were taking place in the focus of activities.

HIID Overseas Projects

The following are a series of projects in seven countries conducted by HIID in its first two years (1974–1976):

1. Bolivia—Ministry of Mines and Metallurgy. Technical assistance on management and tax policies for Bolivia's mining sector. Financed by the World Bank.
2. Iran—the Tehran Development Council. An urban planning project financed by the Government of Iran and the World Bank.
3. Kenya—Ministry of Agriculture. Technical assistance to promote an increase in small–farmer productivity and the decentralization of agricultural development programs. Financed by a consortium of the United Nations and the governments of Canada, the Netherlands, Sweden, the United States, and West Germany.
4. Republic of Korea—the Korea Development Institute. A large research study on the economic and social development of Korea from 1945 to 1975, eventually published in eleven volumes. Financed by the Government of Korea and the U.S. Agency for International Development.
5. Liberia—Ministry of Education. A review of Liberia's educational system providing for continuing involvement of HIID team members through 1976. Financed by USAID.
6. Indonesia—Several new projects including urban development, rural electrification, state bank training, and the Center for Financial Policy Studies and Training. Financed by the Indonesian government.
7. Malaysia—Economic Planning Unit. This was a new project providing for further overseas training, one resident advisor and a number of consultants in the EPU, and two resident advisors in the National Institute of Development Administration. Financed by the U.N. Development Programme.

There was no Ford Foundation financing for any of these projects. The only HIID assistance to planning commissions was the one advisor and a number of consultants to Malaysia's Economic Planning Unit.

The overseas activities of HIID since 1976 have shown a similar range of activities and a similar diversity of sources of finance. In addition to the traditional areas of foreign–exchange and trade policy, technical assistance provided by HIID has tended to concentrate on the following areas: agricultural development, the implementation and management of development programs, training both at home and abroad, taxation and fiscal policy, urban and regional planning, and research. Most of the projects in these fields have called for a multidisciplinary approach in which economists, anthropologists, sociologists, lawyers, and management specialists have been involved.

In the traditional field of monetary, fiscal, and foreign–exchange policy, long cultivated by DAS and HIID, a two–year project in Sri Lanka (1980–82) provided a dozen or more consultants to work on various aspects of government policy in this area. It was financed by the UNDP.

A study of the macro and micro aspects of recurrent cost financing in the Sahel, on the southern fringe of the Sahara, was undertaken jointly with the Centre de Recherche en Développement Économique of the University of Montreal. This study was financed by the Organization for Economic Co-operation and Development by means of a grant from USAID.

In the field of agricultural development, two projects are worthy of mention. The first was the continuation of the large advisory mission to the Ministry of Agriculture in Kenya, financed by a consortium, which was mentioned earlier. The second was a rural development project in the Abyei district of the Sudan, financed by USAID.

During its entire period of existence, HIID has been active in assistance on the implementation and management of development programs and policies. A mission to the African Development Bank was concerned with improving the management of the bank, which was financed by the bank itself. Several projects in Indonesia were of this character, all financed by the Indonesian government. In 1980 the Central Bank of Indonesia asked for help in designing a system for evaluation of a Small Enterprise Credit Program. In the same year the Ministry of Finance asked for help in evaluating four nationwide rural service delivery programs. From 1977 to 1982, HIID was involved in the design and implementation of an experimental program of rural health delivery service in Mali. This was financed by USAID. There were a number of other examples.

HIID has also been engaged in a large number of training programs in Indonesia and elsewhere. These have consisted both in selecting personnel for training abroad and in organizing courses of instruction. One example of the latter was a training program on policy analysis organized in collaboration with various departments of the Indonesian Ministry of Finance and financed by the Indonesian government. Another was a project in Mexico to provide in–house training for the Fundación Javier Barros Sierra A.C., undertaken by Noel McGinn, an Institute Fellow.

Taxation and fiscal policy has been a frequent area of technical assistance. In 1976 a study of mineral taxation was undertaken in

Indonesia, financed by a loan from the World Bank's International Development Association. In 1980 an examination of the possibilities of diversification of tax revenues was undertaken for the Ministry of Finance funded by the Indonesian government.

HIID has undertaken two projects in the area of urban and regional planning. One, already mentioned, was an advisory mission to the Tehran Development Council, concerned with a plan for the City of Tehran, financed by the Government of Iran and the World Bank. The other, undertaken in 1977, involved advice on regional and industrial development of the Guayana region in Venezuela for the Corporación Venezolana de Guayana, financed by that agency.

The largest overseas research assistance provided by HIID was the already–mentioned collaboration with the Korea Development Institute on the study of the modernization of Korea. Assistance was also provided in planning–related research to the Economic Planning Unit of Malaysia. Assistance to the Institute for International Management of the Peoples Republic of China, financed by the U.N. Department of Technical Cooperation for Development in 1981, might also be placed in the research category. It seems likely that overseas research assistance may become an expanding activity for HIID since a number of projects of this sort are now under consideration.

As this is written, in 1985, HIID is heavily engaged overseas in three countries: Indonesia, Kenya, and Bangladesh. In Indonesia there are ten separate projects, mainly concerned with implementation, management, and training. All but one of these projects are financed by the Indonesian government. In Kenya, besides the project with the Ministry of Agriculture, there is another with the Ministry of Finance. The Bangladesh project, although centering on trade and foreign–exchange policy and implementation, covers a wide range of issues. It comes closest of any of the present projects to the older pattern of planning advice. HIID is assisted in the marketing and engineering aspects of the project by collaboration with the Arthur D. Little Corporation of Cambridge. This project is financed by the World Bank.

HIID's Competitive Position

Although HIID is now in good financial shape and adding to its accumulated reserve, its position as an overseas advisory institution is a somewhat precarious one. The shape of the future depends on continuing demand from less developed countries for the services it can provide; on the competition with other agencies capable of providing such services; and on sources of finance. As we have seen, there have been substantial changes in the character of the demand for technical assistance and there will no doubt be further changes. The continued existence of HIID depends in part on its adaptability. The chief competition for HIID comes from profit–seeking consulting institutions and from potential sources of finance such as the World Bank and bilateral assistance agencies capable of providing their own technical assistance. Although HIID has considerable advantages over potential rivals, it is still in a competitive world. As for continued financial support, this depends in part on the ability and willingness of less developed countries themselves to finance such services and, in part, on the continued flow of assistance from bilateral aid programs and from international institutions. Currently the largest group of HIID activities—in Indonesia—is financed in part by oil revenues. There are other oil exporters able to pay for such services, but a promising prospect in Ecuador was cut short because of a change in Ecuador's expectations of foreign–exchange earnings. It seems probable that the flow of bilateral and multilateral assistance to less developed countries will continue and perhaps will increase, but whether HIID will continue to be a preferred channel for technical assistance is perhaps in question. Altogether, though it is an uncertain world, HIID's prospects are not unfavorable.

In 1980, Professor Dwight Perkins of the economics department was named Director of HIID. This was the first time that a tenured member of the Harvard faculty had assumed that position and it marked a large step toward a further integration of the Institute with the Harvard community.

Teaching

As the HIID Biennial Report for 1976–1978 put it:

> In Cambridge, teaching and training programs fall into five categories: (1) formal courses in the various faculties; (2) the development of teaching materials; (3) the placement of project counterpart personnel in U.S. and European universities through the Office of Student Programs; (4) the administration of the

Edward S. Mason Program in Economic Development; and (5) special programs and various seminar series sponsored by HIID.[84]

All of the Institute Fellows and some of the Fellows have regular teaching assignments and spend part of their time when in Cambridge fulfilling these assignments. In 1985–86, there were over 30 courses taught largely or wholly by the HIID staff in the faculties of Arts and Sciences, the Graduate School of Education, the School of Public Health, and the John F. Kennedy School of Government.

The development of teaching materials has been a preoccupation since early in the history of the Development Advisory Service. HIID has carried on this tradition. In 1966, the DAS offered, for the first time, a seminar based on cases derived from overseas experience, and Papanek and his colleagues continued to add to these cases. In 1978, six Institute Fellows and Faculty Fellows, representing five faculties, introduced a half–year graduate course based on a single case that was derived from HIID field projects in Kenya. Michael Roemer and Joseph Stern, utilizing HIID's overseas experience, have published two widely used case books on economic development.[85] Other members of the staff have collected cases in project management, population policy, and health delivery systems and used them in their various courses. In 1983, four members of the staff (Gillis, Perkins, Roemer, and Snodgrass) published a textbook, *Economics of Development*, which is extensively used.[86] Altogether, HIID has made a significant contribution to the preparation of teaching materials.

All of the planning assistance programs of the DAS financed by the Ford Foundation and most of the HIID projects have included financing for the training of host–country personnel overseas. DAS and HIID advisors have helped local institutions identify personnel for whom overseas training is desirable. After nomination by governments, the Office of Student Programs of HIID assists in the selection of programs and institutions appropriate to the candidates' career development, and it arranges admission and monitors academic progress during the period of foreign study. To date, several hundred government officials and prospective officials from countries in which HIID has had projects have been assisted in their studies. Currently, HIID operates a very large program for the overseas training of Indonesian government officials and officials of four large commercial banks.

The Edward S. Mason Program, a joint program of HIID and the John F. Kennedy School of Government, brings to Harvard about 50 carefully selected government officials each year. These mid–career officials are enrolled in an M.P.A. program at the School. In addition to economic development, they study such diverse fields as public management, public enterprise, education and public health planning, and urban and regional planning. This program, originally known as the Public Service Fellows Program, was started on a small scale in 1957 with seven government officials from four countries. In the academic year 1985–86, there were 50 Fellows from 27 countries. HIID interviews more than two hundred candidates a year in their home countries, teaches some of the courses they select, and provides academic and logistical support while the Fellows are resident in Cambridge. By now dozens of former Mason Fellows occupy high positions in their governments' civil service and in political life.

In addition to these teaching activities, HIID continually operates a number of non–credit seminars and workshops for the study of special topics. In 1980, for example, seminars were offered in public enterprise (with the Boston Area Public Enterprise Group), in Indonesian development, and in rural development.

Finally, mention should be made of the mid–career programs for government officials and others run by the Institute. The Public Enterprise Workshop is an eight–week program begun in 1973 with 26 officials in attendance. The tenth session was held in the summer of 1985 with the limit of 40 in attendance. Most of the teaching is undertaken by members of the Boston Area Public Enterprise Group, which includes Boston University, the Massachusetts Institute of Technology, and Harvard. A new workshop, Banking and Monetary Policy in Developing Countries, was started in the summer of 1984 and a third summer workshop, the Program on Investment Appraisal and Management, was initiated in the summer of 1985.

Research

Much of the research of HIID is conducted overseas in connection with policy advice. Examples are the development program implementation studies in Indonesia, the studies of inflation in Malaysia, of recurrent costs in the Sahel, of food policy and rural development in Venezuela, and the numerous studies in Sri Lanka on issues of current development policy. Such studies are normally not published and, because of their relation to contemplated policy action, frequently unpublishable. Nevertheless, they advance the understanding of HIID staff about the development process with repercussions on teaching and advice in other countries.

Including the DAS period, there have been a number of studies of the development process in particular countries in which the organization has been engaged. They have been mentioned earlier—Gustav Papanek on Pakistan, George Baldwin on Iran, Tony Killick on Ghana, Donald Snodgrass on Malaysia, and the eleven volume modernization study of Korea. No doubt there will be more, since HIID has established additional relationships with other overseas research institutions.

Most of the Cambridge-based research, however, tends to be multidisciplinary studies of policy issues encountered in overseas activities. It has produced a large number of published papers and an even larger number of contributions in HIID's Development Discussion Paper series, of which the 187th number was issued in January 1985.[87] As the Triennial Report for 1982–1985 indicates, these papers have tended to concentrate in five broad categories: (1) policy analysis and development administration, including reviews of country experiences; (2) analysis of human capital formation with increasing emphasis on gender and development; (3) analysis of the financial resource mobilization process; (4) the management of public enterprises; and (5) analysis of the optimal use of a nation's natural resources base, including the agricultural sector, and the relationship between natural resource policies and economic growth.

In May 1984, the Director, Dwight Perkins, propounded the question, "How in concrete terms can HIID develop a policy and problems oriented research program over the next five years that is more than the sum of the large number of unrelated articles and an occasional book that are currently being produced?" He thought the answer in part might be found in closer collaboration with research institutes in the less developed countries, but "a research program cannot rely on field projects alone." A way must be found to encourage HIID personnel to collaborate in larger, more significant research. "HIID not only needs to do more collaborative research, it needs to make that research more visible. As work is completed over the next five years, thought will have to go into ways of presenting research results that will have more impact than the present Development Discussion Paper series and *ad hoc* seminars."[88]

Concluding Remarks

Has HIID realized the expectations of those who hoped in 1974 that the scope of advisory, teaching, and research activities of the DAS would be substantially broadened to include disciplines relevant to development other than economics, and that the institution would become a more integral part of the University? And has HIID succeeded in the difficult task of simultaneously serving the interests of the less developed host countries, the University, and the broader world of development studies and communities? In my judgment, the answer is a qualified "yes."

There is no doubt that in its overseas activities the scope of HIID advice has been broadened and the quality of its services improved. It has attained an enviable reputation as a source of professional advice. Its overseas activities have embraced public health delivery services, educational planning, agricultural productivity, urban and regional planning, the management of public enterprises, the implementation of development policies, and other areas relevant to development, but requiring disciplines other than economics. Though there still may be questions concerning the appropriateness of these activities to a University, earlier fears and criticism have diminished.

There is also no doubt that HIID has made large strides in integrating its activities into the normal activities of the University. Its Director is a tenured member of the faculty; most of the courses in development given in the various departments and schools are taught by HIID personnel; and the staff no longer regards itself as extraneous to the normal functions of the University. And overseas experience has thoroughly penetrated the classroom.

It is probably in the area of research that HIID has fallen somewhat short of legitimate expectation. The volume of publication has been large, but it has been scattered and lacking in coherence. It can hardly be said that this research has made a large contribution to an understanding of the development process.

Still, in my view, HIID has justified, if not fully, its creation. It is a unique institution among American and foreign universities and has made Harvard a leading center in the study of the problems of the less developed world.

Notes

1. Dean's Report, Graduate School of Public Administration, 1956–57, p. 466.

2. Despres later went to Stanford University as professor of economics.

3. Keith B. Callard, "Political Focus on Pakistan, 1947–59" (Institute of Pacific Relations, N.Y., 1959), p. 11.

4. This discussion of the Iranian projects is based on my own notes; on a book by George B. Baldwin, a member of the first group of advisors, *Planning and Development in Iran* (Johns Hopkins University Press, Baltimore, 1967); on a manuscript by Thomas McLeod, director of the Second Harvard Advisory Group, "National Planning in Iran, a report based on the experiences of the Harvard Advisory Group in Iran," December 31, 1964; and on a manuscript by Khodadad Farmanfarmaian, Director of the Economic Bureau, "Report [to the Ford Foundation] on Formation and Development of Economic Bureau."

5. Baldwin, *Planning and Development*, p. 183.

6. F. Bjorn Olsen and P. Norregaard Rasmussen, "An Attempt at Planning in a Transitional State," in E.E. Hagen (ed.), *Planning Economic Development* (Homewood, Ill., 1963), p. 249.

7. The Adler Report, mentioned earlier, had suggested that administrative authority be given, at least temporarily, to the foreign advisors. This was unacceptable to Ebtebaj and would have precluded the recruitment of self–respecting Iranians.

8. Farmanfarmaian, Report to the Ford Foundation, supra note 4.

9. Later Dean of the College of Commerce and Business at the University of Saskatchewan. McLeod had been a graduate student of mine at Harvard.

10. Rey Hall, Ford Foundation evaluation of the Iran project.

11. Harvard University Center for International Affairs (CFIA), "The First Five Years, 1958–63," p. 34.

12. These were Richard V. Gilbert, then director of the Pakistan project; William C. Hollinger, who had spent six years overseas in teaching, research, and advisory assignments in Indonesia and Pakistan; Richard D. Mallon, who had spent seven years on the staff of the Economic Commission for Latin America and two years with the Harvard Advisory Group in Pakistan; and Gustav F. Papanek.

13. CFIA, Fourth Annual Report, 1961–62, p. 26–27.

14. Pakistan, Iran, Indonesia, Malaysia, Ghana, Liberia, Ethiopia, Greece, Argentina, and Colombia.

15. CFIA, Eighth Annual Report, 1965–66, p. 22.

16. "A Report to the Ford Foundation of the Committee to Review the Development Advisory Service," March 1971, 60 pp. Typewritten [see note 80 below].

17. Harvard Advisory Group, Pakistan, Progress Report, 1963–64, p. 1.

18. H.A.G., Pakistan, Progress Report, January 1, 1966 – June 30, 1966.

19. H.A.G., Pakistan, Progress Report, 1963–64, p. 1.

20. Ibid., p. 7.

21. This program was the subject of a Ph.D. dissertation at Harvard by John Thomas, then a member of the Harvard Advisory Group in Dacca. Later, as a Development Advisor in Cambridge, Thomas directed a large study for the World Bank on public works programs elsewhere in the less developed world.

22. For a further discussion of these policies, see E. S. Mason, "Economic Development in India and Pakistan," CFIA Occasional Paper #13, September 1966.

23. Gustav Papanek, "Extension and Expansion of the Pakistan Project – when is enough, enough?" May 2, 1967.

24. Ibid.

25. George Rosen, prepublication draft of *Western Economists and Eastern Societies* (Johns Hopkins U. Press, Baltimore, 1985).

26. CFIA, Eighth Annual Report, 1965–66, p. 23.

27. Development Advisory Service, Fifth Annual Report, 1966–67, p. 3–4.

28. Cf. Richard Mallon et al. in Papanek (ed.), *Development Policy: Theory and Practice* (Harvard University Press, 1968).

29. Richard D. Mallon, personal communication, 1985.

30. Richard D. Mallon with Juan V. Sourrouille, *Economic policymaking in a conflict society, The argentine case.* Cambridge, MA: Harvard University Press, 1975. [English].

Richard D. Mallon y Juan Sourrouille, *La pólitica económica en una sociedad conflictiva. El caso argentino*, Biblioteca de economía política, Amorrortu editores, Buenos Aires, 1973. [Spanish]. Sourrouille later served as Secretary of Planning and then Minister of the Economy under President Raul Alfonsín.

31. DAS, Fifth Annual Report, 1966–67, page 4.

32. Quoted in report of Harvard Advisory Group, Colombia, for October–December 1969.

33. K. N. Rao, "Evaluation of Grants in Support of the National Planning Department of Colombia," November 7, 1983.

34. R. D. Mallon, "Report on the New Approach of the DAS," September 25, 1970.

35. Rao, "Evaluation," 1983.

36. Report on Liberia, December 5, 1967.

37. Ibid. Of course that would not be saying a great deal.

38. Lester Gordon, Memorandum, 1967.

39. "An Informal Report on the Greek Project," August 1966.

40. Ibid.

41. This is taken from my diary.

42. Letter dated August 16, 1967.

43. Letter from P. D. Henderson to Lester Gordon.

44. "Report on a Potential Ghana Project," December 13, 1966.

45. Tony Killick, *Development Economics in Action: A Study of Economic Policies in Ghana* (Heinemann, London, 1978). Killick was a member of the Harvard team in Ghana during the second stage of the project. From 1961 to 1965 he had served on the faculty of the University of Ghana and he is currently director of the Overseas Development Council in London. I have relied heavily on his account.

46. Leslie E. Grayson, "The Role of Suppliers" Credit in the Industrialization of Ghana," *Economic Development and Cultural Change*, April 1973, p. 429. Grayson, who was a member of the first Harvard team in Ghana, describes the procedure, p. 488.

47. Papanek continued: "The equipment peddler sells the equipment and the buying country – all of Ghana's suppliers' credits went to public entities – contracts to repay the price of equipment over a period of time. The peddler there obtains credit from private banks and has it guaranteed by his own country's government export credit insurance organization. Once this is accomplished any future dealings that the LDC governments have are not with the equipment peddler but with the exporting country's credit insurance organization." The credit–supplying countries are not free of blame for many of the white elephants and loss–making public enterprises not only in Ghana but in other African countries.

48. Report on Ghana, December 5, 1967.

49. Report by J. Koopman, February–July, 1968.

50. Gustav Papanek.

51. DAS Tenth Annual Report for 1971–72.

52. These stirring events are related in a paper by advisors Tony Killick, Michael Roemer, and Joseph J. Stern, "Devaluation of the Coup d'Etat in Ghana" (September 1972), p. 38. They preface this paper by maxim 149 of Publius Syrus, "Many receive advice, few profit from it."

53. Quoted in Killick, *Development Economics in Action*, p. 299.

54. Milton J. Esman, *Administration and Development in Malaysia* (Cornell U. Press, Ithaca, N.Y., 1972), p. 4.

55. Donald R. Snodgrass, *Inequality and Economic Development in Malaysia* (Oxford University Press, 1980), p. 141. Snodgrass was an advisor to EPU from 1964–1966 and joined the Harvard project as a Development Advisor in 1968, where he remained until 1972.

56. Ibid., p. 47.

57. "Development Administration in Malaysia: Report to the Government of Malaysia" (Government Printer, Kuala Lampur, 1966).

58. Milton J. Esman, memorandum dated January 17, 1967.

59. Snodgrass, *Inequality*, p. 197.

60. Letter to Lester Gordon, Director of DAS, May 17, 1969.

61. Letter to Lester Gordon, May 19, 1969.

62. On this see Bruce Glassburner, "Economic Policy after Sukarno," in Glassburner (ed.), *The Economy of Indonesia* (Cornell U. Press, Ithaca, N.Y., 1971), p. 433.

63. Benjamin Higgins, *Economic Development*, revised edition. (W. W. Norton, N.Y. 1968), p. 678.

64. H.A.G., Indonesia, Report, July 1, 1968 to June 30, 1969.

65. Ibid.

66. Ibid.

67. DAS Eighth Annual Report, 1969–70, p. 10.

68. H.A.G., Indonesia, Report, January–June 1972.

69. Papanek Report of February 2, 1970.

70. Report of UNDP Mission, April 1970.

71. DAS Tenth Annual Report, July 1, 1971 to June 30, 1972.

72. CFIA, Eighth Annual Report, 1965–66, p. 25.

73. Final Report on the Operation of the Development Advisory Service, July 1, 1972 to June 30, 1974, p. 20–24.

74. HIID, "The First Two Years, 1974–76," p. 30.

75. Korean Modernization series.

76. DAS Final Report, 1972–74.

77. Memo from Carl Gotsch to DAS Advisory Committee, May 27, 1970.

78. Tour notes March 18, 1971.

79. "Report of the Ad Hoc Committee to Review the Development Advisory Service," October 1969, Robert Dorfman, chairman (Economics); Francis Bator (Kennedy School); Milton Katz (Law School); Seymour Lipset (Social Relations); Richard Neustadt (Kennedy School); Edwin Reischauer (East Asian Studies).

80. "A Report to the Ford Foundation of the Committee to Review the Development Advisory Service," March 1971, 60 pp. typewritten. The committee members were Stephen Lewis (Williams), Carlos Diaz (Yale), and Edgar Edwards (of the Foundation), all of whom had had considerable experience in the development area. The committee took their assignment seriously, visiting three of the overseas projects and interviewing some 60 DAS members, University staff, and host government officials. All of the direct quotes that follow in this section are from this same source.

81. "International Development at Harvard: Proposed New International Arrangements," July 19, 1973, typed.

82. "Document Approved by the President and Fellows of Harvard University in Establishing HIID," Annex A.

83. HIID Biennial Report, 1978–80, p. 1.

84. HIID Biennial Report, 1976–78.

85. *An Appraisal of Development Projects: A Practical Guide to Project Analysis with Case Studies and Solutions* (Praeger, N.Y., 1975); and *Cases in Economic Development: Projects, Policies and Strategies*, (Butterworth, London, 1981).

86. Gillis, Perkins, Roemer, and Snodgrass.

87. This monograph was initially issued as Development Discussion Paper No. 187. By the end of 1985 the number of DDPs had grown to 212.

88. Dwight Perkins, Five–Year Plan, 1984–1989, Harvard Institute for International Development, Cambridge, August 1984, p. 19–20.

Appendix A: Long-Term Advisors to Overseas Projects, 1954–1985

Advisor, (*Nationality*)
HIID Overseas Assignment

William I. Abraham, (*U.S.A.*)
Bangladesh
Ethiopia
J. James Ackroyd, (*U.S.A.*)
Sudan
Hans Adler, (*U.S.A.*)
Pakistan
Timothy Aldington, (*U.K.*)
Kenya
*Lascelles Anderson, (*U.S.A.*)
Liberia
Walton J. Anderson, (*Canada*)
Ghana
Carl Anonsen, (*Norway*)
Liberia
Oddvar Aresvik, (*Norway*)
Pakistan
George B. Baldwin, (*U.S.A.*)
Iran
Heinz Bachmann, (*Switzerland*)
Liberia
Richard M. Barkay, (*Israel*)
Liberia
Vincent M. Barnett, Jr., (*U.S.A.*)
Malaysia
Alan Batchelder, (*U.S.A.*)
Liberia
Avery Batson, (*U.S.A.*)
Pakistan
Jacques Baudouy, (*France*)
Mali
Ralph Beals, (*U.S.A.*)
Indonesia
*David E. Bell, (*U.S.A.*)
Pakistan
Beryl Bellman, (*U.S.A.*)
Liberia
*Elliot J. Berg, (*U.S.A.*)
Liberia

Advisor, (*Nationality*)
HIID Overseas Assignment

Asbjorn Bergan, (*Norway*)
Pakistan
Forrest Berkley, (*U.S.A.*)
Indonesia
Klaus W. Bethke, (*Colombia*)
Kenya
*Richard M. Bird, (*Canada*)
Colombia
Petter J. Bjerve, (*Norway*)
Pakistan
Donald J. Blake, (*U.S.A.*)
Indonesia
Bruce Bolnick, (*U.S.A.*)
Indonesia
Paul Booz, (*U.S.A.*)
Pakistan
Wilhelm Boucherie, (*Germany*)
Indonesia
Gerard Boulch, (*France*)
Ivory Coast
William Breda, (*U.S.A.*)
Pakistan
Frederick S. Brooman, (*U.K.*)
Argentina
John Brower, (*U.S.A.*)
Bolivia
M. W. Bocuvetsky, (*Canada*)
Bolivia
Robert E. Burns, (*U.S.A.*)
Ethiopia
Pakistan
Leslie M. Burgess, (*U.S.A.*)
Pakistan
Willem C. F. Bussink, (*Netherlands*)
Pakistan
Ann H. Byerly, (*U.S.A.*)
Sudan
John Cairncross, (*U.K.*)
Pakistan

Advisor, (*Nationality*) HIID Overseas Assignment
Loel Callahan, (*U.S.A.*)
Mali
Harry L. Case, (*U.S.A.*)
Pakistan
Phillip Chantler, (*U.S.A.*)
Pakistan
Giles Chitty, (*U.K.*)
Indonesia
Paul G. Clark, (*U.S.A.*)
Malaysia
*John M. Cohen, (*U.S.A.*)
Kenya
*David C. Cole, (*U.S.A.*)
Indonesia
Michael Cole, (*U.S.A.*)
Liberia
Edward N. Cooper, (*U.S.A.*)
Pakistan
Achsah Coursen, (*U.S.A.*)
Liberia
Ralph W. Cummings, Jr., (*U.S.A.*)
Indonesia
Clifford D. Curtis, (*Canada*)
Pakistan
David O. Dapice, (*U.S.A.*)
Indonesia
Nils M. P. Daulaire, (*U.S.A.*)
Mali
Robert Davenport, (*U.S.A.*)
Indonesia
Dirk Jan Dekker, (*Netherlands*)
Liberia
John W. Delaplaine, (*U.S.A.*)
Colombia
H. Peter Delp, (*U.S.A.*)
Kenya
Gieuseppe DeSole, (*Italy*)
Mali
Emile Despres, (*U.S.A.*)
Pakistan
John Diamond, (*U.K.*)
Malaysia

Advisor, (*Nationality*) HIID Overseas Assignment
Jakob H. Diddens, (*Netherlands*)
Liberia
Malaysia
Pakistan
Ion Dimitriou, (*Greece*)
Pakistan
William Dodge, (*U.S.A.*)
Ethiopia
William Donovan, (*U.S.A.*)
Sudan
Christopher Dougherty, (*U.K.*)
Colombia
Jerome Doutriaux, (*France*)
Venezuela
J. Kamal Dow, (*U.S.A.*)
Kenya
Constantin A. Doxiades, (*Greece*)
Pakistan
Robert S. Drysdale, (*Canada*)
Colombia
Harold B. Dunkerley, (*U.K.*)
Colombia
Ghana
John C. Eddison, (*U.S.A.*)
Colombia
Pakistan
Z. A. M. Eltezam, (*Afghanistan*)
Bangladesh
Eivind Erichsen, (*Norway*)
Pakistan
Jan Erichson, (*Sweden*)
Kenya
Milton J. Esman, (*U.S.A.*)
Malaysia
Hugh E. Evans, (*U.S.A.*)
Kenya
Just Faaland, (*Norway*)
Malaysia
Pakistan
Walter P. Falcon, (*U.S.A.*)
Pakistan

Advisor, (*Nationality*)
HIID Overseas Assignment

David Feldman, (*U.K.*)
Kenya
Jorgen A. H. Fenger, (*Denmark*)
Liberia
Pakistan
Frank Flatters, (*Canada*)
Indonesia
Stephen A. Freeman, (*U.S.A.*)
Iran
Remy T. Freire, (*Brazil*)
Argentina
Richard Fuller, (*U.S.A.*)
Sudan
Richard Funkhouser, (*U.S.A.*)
Indonesia
Harry Garnett, (*U.K.*)
Iran
William B. Gates, Jr., (*U.S.A.*)
Malaysia
Judith K. Geist, (*U.S.A.*)
Kenya
Elon H. Gilbert, (*U.S.A.*)
Ghana
Richard V. Gilbert, (*U.S.A.*)
Indonesia
Pakistan
*S. Malcolm Gillis, (*U.S.A.*)
Bolivia
Indonesia
Theodore J. Goering, (*U.S.A.*)
Ethiopia
Malaysia
*Richard H. Goldman, (*U.S.A.*)
Kenya
*Lester E. Gordon, (*U.S.A.*)
Kenya
*Carl H. Gotsch, (*U.S.A.*)
Pakistan
*Cheryl Williamson Gray, (*U.S.A.*)
Indonesia
*Clive S. Gray, (*U.S.A.*)
Colombia
Ethiopia
Indonesia

Advisor, (*Nationality*)
HIID Overseas Assignment

Leslie E. Grayson, (*U.S.A.*)
Ghana
Wade Gregory, (*U.S.A.*)
Kenya
Stephen Gulick, (*U.S.A.*)
Sudan
Rolf Gusten, (*Germany*)
Liberia
G. O. Gutman, (*Australia*)
Pakistan
Paul Haddow, (*Canada*)
Kenya
Malcolm Hall, (*U.K.*)
Ivory Coast
Kenya
Fred Hanga, Jr., (*U.S.A.*)
Iran
Liberia
Kenneth R. Hansen, (*U.S.A.*)
Iran
Poul Buch Hansen, (*Denmark*)
Liberia
Stein Hansen, (*Norway*)
Iran
David Harman, (*Israel*)
Liberia
Samuel Harmon, (*U.S.A.*)
Kenya
David Harner, (*U.S.A.*)
Malaysia
S. F. Harris, (*Australia*)
Colombia
Everett D. Hawkins, (*U.S.A.*)
Indonesia
P. David Henderson, (*U.K.*)
Greece
Malaysia
James B. Hendry, (*U.S.A.*)
Pakistan
Melvin Hendry, (*U.S.A.*)
Liberia

Advisor, (*Nationality*)
HIID Overseas Assignment

Ole Bus Henriksen, (*Denmark*)
Indonesia
J. Tomas Hexner, (*U.S.A.*)
Pakistan
John E. Hirten, (*U.S.A.*)
Iran
Oscar Donald Hoerr, (*U.S.A.*)
Ethiopia
Malaysia
Lutz Hoffmann, (*W. Germany*)
Malaysia
Flora Hollinger, (*U.S.A.*)
Liberia
William C. Hollinger, (*U.S.A.*)
Indonesia
Liberia
Pakistan
David Holmes, (*U.S.A.*)
Venezuela
Richard M. Hook, (*U.S.A.*)
Kenya
Thiri Pyanchi Hpu, (*Burma*)
Pakistan
Gary C. Hufbauer, (*U.S.A.*)
Pakistan
W. Richard Huntington, (*U.S.A.*)
Sudan
Thomas L. Hutcheson, (*U.S.A.*)
Bangladesh
Colombia
Nils-Ivar Isaksson, (*Sweden*)
Kenya
Cathy L. Jabara, (*U.S.A.*)
Kenya
Hans J. Jaksch, (*Germany*)
Colombia
Frank G. Jarrett, (*Australia*)
Pakistan
*Glenn P. Jenkins, (*Canada*)
Bolivia
Malaysia
Alan G. Johnston, (*U.S.A.*)
Kenya

Advisor, (*Nationality*)
HIID Overseas Assignment

*Leroy Jones, (*U.S.A.*)
Korea
Lars G. Kalderen, (*Sweden*)
Ethiopia
Wolfgang Kasper, (*Germany*)
Malaysia
Douglas H. Keare, (*U.S.A.*)
Malaysia
Albert Keidel, (*U.S.A.*)
Korea
Patrick Kelly, (*U.S.A.*)
Mali
Roy B. Kelly, (*U.S.A.*)
Indonesia
James R. Kern, (*U.S.A.*)
Indonesia
Thomas Kerr, (*Canada*)
Kenya
*Maurice Kilbridge, (*U.S.A.*)
Pakistan
Anthony J. Killick, (*U.K.*)
Ghana
Jack Knetsch, (*U.S.A.*)
Malaysia
Joop Koopman, Jr., (*Netherlands*)
Colombia
Pakistan
Jozeph Koopman, (*Netherlands*)
Ghana
Mark LaPointe, (*U.S.A.*)
Mali
Dana Larsen, (*U.S.A.*)
Sudan
Karsten Laursen, (*Denmark*)
Colombia
Svend Laursen, (*U.S.A.*)
Pakistan
David K. Leonard, (*U.S.A.*)
Kenya
Claude Letarte, (*Canada*)
Mali
David B. Lewis, (*U.S.A.*)
Kenya

Advisor, (*Nationality*)
HIID Overseas Assignment

J. N. Lewis, (*Australia*)
Pakistan
Theodore Liebman, (*U.S.A.*)
Iran
Millard Long, (*U.S.A.*)
Pakistan
Marinus Maasland, (*U.S.A.*)
Pakistan
Ian MacArthur, (*Australia*)
Kenya
Alasdair I. MacBean, (*U.K.*)
Pakistan
Athole S. Mackintosh, (*U.K.*)
Pakistan
Angus Maddison, (*U.K.*)
Ghana
Pakistan
*Richard D. Mallon, (*U.S.A.*)
Argentina
Bangladesh
Colombia
Nicaragua
Pakistan
Kurt Martin, (*U.K.*)
Ghana
Indonesia
Iran
Lee Martin, (*U.S.A.*)
Pakistan
Geoffrey W. Maynard, (*U.K.*)
Argentina
David S. McCauley, (*U.S.A.*)
Indonesia
Iain McDonald, (*Australia*)
Kenya
Lloyd E. McKay, (*Australia*)
Bangladesh
*Noel F. McGinn, (*U.S.A.*)
Liberia
Mexico
Joseph McGovern, (*U.S.A.*)
Kenya

Advisor, (*Nationality*)
HIID Overseas Assignment

Malcolm F. McPherson, (*Australia*)
The Gambia
W. W. McPherson, (*U.S.A.*)
Pakistan
Donald Mead, (*U.S.A.*)
Ethiopia
Leon A. Mears, (*U.S.A.*)
Indonesia
Pakistan
Max Medley, (*U.S.A.*)
Malaysia
Jacob Meerman, (*U.S.A.*)
Liberia
Ronald Mendelsohn, (*Australia*)
Iran
Bengt Metelius, (*Sweden*)
Colombia
Richard Meyers, (*U.S.A.*)
Kenya
Sijb'ren Miedema, (*Netherlands*)
Ghana
Richard T. Monteverde, (*U.S.A.*)
Indonesia
David Morawetz, (*Australia*)
Colombia
Morris Moses, (*U.S.A.*)
Argentina
Joseph Motherall, (*U.S.A.*)
Pakistan
Alberto R. Musalem, (*Argentina*)
Colombia
Courtney A. Nelson, (*U.S.A.*)
Indonesia
Eric R. Nelson, (*U.S.A.*)
Indonesia
Maryam Niamir, (*Iran*)
Sudan
Stanley A. Nicholson, (*U.S.A.*)
Colombia
Bjorn Nilson, (*U.S.A.*)
Mali

Advisor, (*Nationality*)
HIID Overseas Assignment

Ole David Koht Norbye, (*Norway*)
Bangladesh
Pakistan
Timothy Nulty, (*U.S.A.*)
Pakistan
Arne Oien, (*Norway*)
Pakistan
Anders Olgaard, (*Denmark*)
Malaysia
Harlow Osborne, (*U.S.A.*)
Venezuela
Theodore K. Osgood, (*U.S.A.*)
Malaysia
Richard B. Pagett, (*U.S.A.*)
Indonesia
Romano Pantanali, (*Italy*)
Ghana
*Gustav F. Papanek, (*U.S.A.*)
Indonesia
Pakistan
Stephen Parker, (*U.S.A.*)
Indonesia
Earl Partenheimer, (*U.S.A.*)
Kenya
Richard H. Patten, (*U.S.A.*)
Ghana
Indonesia
Pakistan
Brian B. Perkins, (*U.K.*)
Colombia
Joseph Phillips, (*U.S.A.*)
Argentina
A. Kenneth Pickering, (*U.K.*)
Indonesia
Pakistan
Thomas C. Pinckney III, (*U.S.A.*)
Kenya
Robert J. Pogson, (*U.S.A.*)
Iran
Liberia
Richard C. Porter, (*U.S.A.*)
Colombia
Indonesia

Advisor, (*Nationality*)
HIID Overseas Assignment

James Prescott, (*U.S.A.*)
Iran
S. Ramakrishnan, (*India*)
Kenya
W. Brian Reddaway, (*U.K.*)
Ghana
D. Gene Reese, (*U.S.A.*)
Pakistan
*Robert Repetto, (*U.S.A.*)
Pakistan
Robert C. Rice, (*U.S.A.*)
Tanzania
Hamlin Robinson, (*U.S.A.*)
Malaysia
Marguerite S. Robinson, (*U.S.A.*)
Indonesia
Emery M. Roe, (*U.S.A.*)
Kenya
*Michael Roemer, (*U.S.A.*)
Ghana
Kenya
Tanzania
Evan R. Rotner, (*U.S.A.*)
Pakistan
Hans Ruthenberg, (*Germany*)
Kenya
Olaf Saetersdal, (*Norway*)
Colombia
Nicaragua
Roberto Salomon, (*Argentina*)
Nicaragua
Venezuela
W. E. G. Salter, (*Australia*)
Pakistan
Robert Sarly, (*U.S.A.*)
Iran
Josef Scheider, (*U.S.A.*)
Pakistan
Daniel Schydlowsky, (*Peru*)
Argentina

Advisor, (*Nationality*)
HIID Overseas Assignment

Gerald Scully, (*U.S.A.*)
Iran
Roger Selley, (*U.S.A.*)
Ghana
Lalit K. Sen, (*India*)
Indonesia
Charles Shapiro, (*U.S.A.*)
Iran
Joseph G. Sharp, Jr., (*U.S.A.*)
Sudan
Jennifer Sharpley, (*Australia*)
Kenya
Michael J. Sharpston, (*U.K.*)
Ghana
Carroll K. Shaw, (*U.S.A.*)
Malaysia
Edward S. Shaw, (*U.S.A.*)
Ghana
John B. Sheahan, (*U.S.A.*)
Colombia
Fred Shorter, (*U.S.A.*)
Pakistan
Pavle Sicherl, (*Yugoslavia*)
Ethiopia
Theodore R. Smith, (*U.S.A.*)
Indonesia
Malaysia
*Donald R. Snodgrass, (*U.S.A.*)
Indonesia
Malaysia
J. Herbert Snyder, (*U.S.A.*)
Pakistan
Wayne W. Snyder, (*U.S.A.*)
Indonesia
Lorne Sonely, (*U.S.A.*)
Iran
William Steel, (*U.S.A.*)
Ivory Coast
*Joseph J. Stern, (*U.S.A.*)
Ghana
Malaysia
Pakistan

Advisor, (*Nationality*)
HIID Overseas Assignment

*Kenneth Swanberg, (*U.S.A.*)
Kenya
Edward F. Szczepanik, (*U.K.*)
Pakistan
Carol A. Taylor, (*U.S.A.*)
Colombia
*Lester D. Taylor, (*U.S.A.*)
Colombia
Mary Taylor, (*U.S.A.*)
Mali
Andrew Tench, (*U.K.*)
Kenya
Alexander ter Weele, (*U.S.A.*)
Ethiopia
Johanes Th. Thijsse, (*Netherlands*)
Pakistan
*John W. Thomas, (*U.S.A.*)
Kenya
Pakistan
Philip S. Thomas, (*U.S.A.*)
Pakistan
Bo E. Thome, (*Sweden*)
Ethiopia
Niels C. Thygesen, (*Denmark*)
Malaysia
Gene M. Tidrick, (*U.S.A.*)
Tanzania
*C. Peter Timmer, (*U.S.A.*)
Indonesia
Wouter Tims, (*Netherlands*)
Pakistan
Sadik Toksoz, (*Turkey*)
Kenya
Stephen G. Triantis, (*Canada*)
Greece
Per S. Tveite, (*Norway*)
Pakistan
Malcolm Urquhart, (*Canada*)
Pakistan
Constantine V. Vaitsos, (*Greece*)
Colombia

Advisor, (*Nationality*)
HIID Overseas Assignment

Franklin D. Van Buer, (*U.S.A.*)
Kenya
W. H. van den Toorn, (*Netherlands*)
Kenya
Willy van Rijckeghem, (*Belgium*)
Argentina
Robert C. G. Varley, (*U.K.*)
Indonesia
Kandaswamy Venkatesan, (*India*)
Kenya
Georges Vernez, (*Switzerland*)
Colombia
Nicaragua
Eben Walker, (*U.S.A.*)
Indonesia
Robert W. Warner, (*Australia*)
Bangladesh
Bernard Wasow, (*U.S.A.*)
Bangladesh
Peter F. Weisel, (*U.S.A.*)
Liberia
*Louis T. Wells, Jr., (*U.S.A.*)
Bolivia
Clay G. Wescott, (*U.S.A.*)
Kenya
Michael Westlake, (*U.K.*)
Kenya
Lawrence J. White, (*U.S.A.*)
Pakistan
David Williams, (*Australia*)
Bolivia
Ghana
Tanzania
Douglas Windham, (*U.S.A.*)
Liberia
Daniel Wisecarver, (*U.S.A.*)
Bolivia
Brian Wright, (*Australia*)
Bolivia
Jean B. Wyckoff, (*U.S.A.*)
Kenya
Craig J. Wynn, (*U.S.A.*)
Sudan
Carlos Zulberti, (*Argentina*)
Kenya

* Indicates persons who held Harvard corporation appointments at the rank of Instructor or above during or after their DAS/HIID service.

Appendix B: Short-Term Consultants to Overseas Projects, 1954–1985

Consultant, (*Nationality*)
HIID Overseas Assignment

William I. Abraham, (*U.S.A.*)
Indonesia
Kenya
Malaysia
John Adler, (*U.S.A.*)
Venezuela
A. M. S. Ahmad, (*Pakistan*)
Indonesia
Junaid Kamal Ahmad, (*Bangladesh*)
Bangladesh
Polly Allen, (*U.S.A.*)
Indonesia
*Alice H. Amsden, (*U.S.A.*)
Bangladesh
Fuat Andic, (*Turkey*)
Malaysia
*Lascelles Anderson, (*U.S.A.*)
Liberia
*Peter S. Ashton, (*U.K.*)
Indonesia
Henry Aubrey, (*U.S.A.*)
Pakistan
Roy Bahl, (*U.S.A.*)
Korea
Robert E. Baldwin, (*U.S.A.*)
Indonesia
Molly Bang–Campbell, (*U.S.A.*)
Mali
Richard M. Barkay, (*Israel*)
Liberia
Vincent Lewis Bassie, (*U.S.A.*)
Colombia
Alan Batchelder, (*U.S.A.*)
Malaysia
Merrill J. Bateman, (*U.S.A.*)
Ghana
Ralph Beals, (*U.S.A.*)
Indonesia
Martin Beckman, (*U.S.A.*)
Iran

Consultant, (*Nationality*)
HIID Overseas Assignment

Michael E. Beesley, (*U.K.*)
Pakistan
Jere R. Behrman, (*U.S.A.*)
Nicaragua
Cody W. Benjamin, (*U.S.A.*)
Sudan
Kwamena Bentsi–Enchill, (*Ghana*)
Liberia
*Elliot J. Berg, (*U.S.A.*)
Sahel
*Brian J. L. Berry, (*U.S.A.*)
Indonesia
Iran
R. Albert Berry, (*U.S.A.*)
Venezuela
Glenn G. Bingham, (*U.S.A.*)
Indonesia
Tyler S. Biggs, (*U.S.A.*)
Dominican Republic
*Richard Bird, (*Canada*)
Indonesia
*John Black, (*U.S.A.*)
Pakistan
Charles Blitzer, (*U.S.A.*)
Ecuador
Rae Blumberg, (*U.S.A.*)
Venezuela
Jack Boorman, (*U.S.A.*)
Indonesia
Wassalke Bonkau, (*Niger*)
Sahel
Fredi Bove, (*U.S.A.*)
Sahel
*John R. Bowen, (*U.S.A.*)
Indonesia
*Samuel Bowles, (*U.S.A.*)
Greece
Roy Brady, (*U.K.*)
Iran

Consultant, (*Nationality*)
HIID Overseas Assignment

*Vincent Brandt, (*U.S.A.*)
Korea
Lawrence Bridge, (*U.S.A.*)
Venezuela
Derick Brinkerhoff, (*U.S.A.*)
Mali
*John Brode, (*U.S.A.*)
Bangladesh
Keith Brodie, (*U.S.A.*)
Sudan
John Brotchie, (*Australia*)
Iran
Michael Bruno, (*Israel*)
Greece
Henry J. Bruton, (*U.S.A.*)
Korea
Malaysia
Warren Bull, (*Canada*)
Indonesia
Robert E. Burns, (*U.S.A.*)
Colombia
Matthew A. Cameron, (*U.K.*)
Pakistan
Daniel O. Cantor, (*U.S.A.*)
Kenya
John Copeland, (*U.S.A.*)
Indonesia
Roberto Carreto, (*Mexico*)
Venezuela
John Carroll, (*U.S.A.*)
Indonesia
*Richard A. Cash, (*U.S.A.*)
Mali
Sudan
John Chant, (*Canada*)
Indonesia
William R. Charleson, (*U.S.A.*)
Argentina
*Hollis B. Chenery, (*U.S.A.*)
Pakistan
James Clad, (*New Zealand*)
Indonesia
William R. Claybaugh, (*U.S.A.*)
Sudan

Consultant, (*Nationality*)
HIID Overseas Assignment

Sijbren Cnossen, (*Netherlands*)
Indonesia
*John M. Cohen, (*U.S.A.*)
Sudan
Kenya
*David C. Cole, (*U.S.A.*)
China
Indonesia
Kenya
Korea
Sri Lanka
Sudan
Venezuela
*Alfred H. Conrad, (*U.S.A.*)
Argentina
Ghana
Liberia
Pakistan
*Robert F. Conrad, (*U.S.A.*)
Ecuador
Indonesia
John G. Corina, (*U.K.*)
Argentina
Edward Craft, (*U.S.A.*)
Indonesia
Keith G. Crellin, (*Australia*)
Indonesia
William K. Cummings, (*U.S.A.*)
Indonesia
*Charles T. W. (Adam) Curle, (*U.K.*)
Liberia
Pakistan
Belden H. Daniels, (*U.S.A.*)
Indonesia
*Andre Daniere, (*U.S.A.*)
Sahel
David O. Dapice, (*U.S.A.*)
Indonesia
Robert W. Davenport, (*U.S.A.*)
Indonesia
Kenneth Davey, (*U.K.*)
Indonesia
*Russell G. Davis, (*U.S.A.*)
Argentina

Consultant, (*Nationality*)
HIID Overseas Assignment

Edgar W. Davy, (*U.S.A.*)
Korea
Edmond de Gaiffier, (*Belgium*)
Indonesia
Lawrence Delliquadu, (*U.S.A.*)
Mali
H. Peter Delp, (*U.S.A.*)
Kenya
Laketeh Derasse, (*Ethiopia*)
Kenya
Pieter de Wolff, (*Netherlands*)
Argentina
M. Mamadou Diouf, (*Senegal*)
Sahel
Oldrich Dittrich, (*U.S.A.*)
Venezuela
*William A. Doebele, (*U.S.A.*)
Indonesia
*Robert Dorfman, (*U.S.A.*)
Ghana
Indonesia
Korea
Pakistan
Peter Dorner, (*U.S.A.*)
Ethiopia
Jerome A. Doutriaux, (*France*)
Venezuela
Ian M. Drummond, (*Canada*)
Colombia
Jean Due, (*U.S.A.*)
Indonesia
John Due, (*U.S.A.*)
Indonesia
*James S. Duesenberry, (*U.S.A.*)
Indonesia
Sri Lanka
Richard Durstine, (*U.S.A.*)
Argentina
Bruce R. F. Eaton, (*Canada*)
Sudan
John C. Edmunds, (*U.S.A.*)
Kenya
Sebastian Edwards, (*Chile*)
Indonesia

Consultant, (*Nationality*)
HIID Overseas Assignment

Marcial Echenique, (*U.K.*)
Iran
Just Faaland, (*Norway*)
Pakistan
*Merle G. Fainsod, (*U.S.A.*)
Malaysia
*Walter P. Falcon, (*U.S.A.*)
Indonesia
Malaysia
Pakistan
David Felix, (*U.S.A.*)
Argentina
Marilyn Fetterman, (*U.S.A.*)
Sudan
Jonathan Fisher, (*U.S.A.*)
Sudan
Paul Fisher, (*Austria*)
Korea
Frank Flatters, (*Canada*)
Indonesia
Anthony Flowerdew, (*U.K.*)
Iran
Dominique Fougerouse, (*France*)
Mali
*James J. Fox, (*U.S.A.*)
Indonesia
*Richard C. Freeman, (*U.S.A.*)
Sri Lanka
Jerome Fried, (*U.S.A.*)
Iran
Lina M. Fruzzetti, (*Ethiopia*)
Sudan
Maxwell Fry, (*U.K.*)
Indonesia
Victor Fung, (*Hong Kong*)
Indonesia
Sulayman Fye, (*The Gambia*)
Sahel
Alfonso Gadia, (*Philippines*)
Indonesia
*John K. Galbraith, (*U.S.A.*)
Colombia
Pakistan
George Gant, (*U.S.A.*)
Pakistan

Consultant, (*Nationality*)
HIID Overseas Assignment

Alexander Ganz, (*U.S.A.*)
Venezuela
Peter Gardiner, (*U.S.A.*)
Indonesia
Monique Garrity, (*U.S.A.*)
Sahel
William B. Gates, (*U.S.A.*)
Indonesia
James Gavan, (*U.S.A.*)
Peru
Judith K. Geist, (*U.S.A.*)
Kenya
Joan Gerrity, (*U.S.A.*)
Indonesia
Jerrold Gibson, (*U.S.A.*)
Indonesia
Andrew F. Giffin, (*U.S.A.*)
Indonesia
*S. Malcolm Gillis, (*U.S.A.*)
Bolivia
Colombia
Ecuador
Ghana
Indonesia
J. Price Gittinger, (*U.S.A.*)
Iran
Kangethe Gitu, (*Kenya*)
Kenya
Bernard Gladieux, (*U.S.A.*)
Pakistan
*Nathan Glazer, (*U.S.A.*)
Malaysia
Graham Glenday, (*Canada*)
Indonesia
Ricardo A. Godoy, (*U.S.A.*)
Indonesia
Max Goldensohn, (*U.S.A.*)
Mali
*Richard H. Goldman, (*U.S.A.*)
Indonesia
Kenya
Malaysia
Sri Lanka

Consultant, (*Nationality*)
HIID Overseas Assignment

Mauro Gonzalez–Luna, (*Mexico*)
Indonesia
William Goodman, (*U.S.A.*)
Iran
Gerry Goodrich, (*U.S.A.*)
Mali
*Lester E. Gordon, (*U.S.A.*)
Indonesia
Kenya
*Carl H. Gotsch, (*U.S.A.*)
Kenya
Gordon K. Goundrey, (*Canada*)
Liberia
*Clive S. Gray, (*U.S.A.*)
Mali
Sahel
Somalia
Venezuela
Dale Gray, (*U.S.A.*)
Indonesia
C. Robinson Gregory, (*U.S.A.*)
Liberia
Daniel L. Gressel, (*U.S.A.*)
Indonesia
Merilee S. Grindle, (*U.S.A.*)
Dominican Republic
Alieto Guadagni, (*Argentina*)
Venezuela
Yves Guerard, (*Canada*)
Indonesia
Stephen Guisinger, (*U.S.A.*)
Ethiopia
Odd Gulbrandsen, (*Norway*)
Pakistan
John G. Gurley, (*U.S.A.*)
Indonesia
Michael Hanrahan, (*U.S.A.*)
Kenya
Kenneth R. Hansen, (*U.S.A.*)
Iran
Arnold C. Harberger, (*U.S.A.*)
Colombia
Indonesia
Venezuela

Consultant, (*Nationality*)
HIID Overseas Assignment

J. Ross Harding, (*Australia*)
Malaysia
Thomas Hart, (*U.S.A.*)
Indonesia
*David Hartman, (*U.S.A.*)
Indonesia
Jonathan Haughton, (*Ireland*)
Sahel
Jane J. Hayes, (*U.S.A.*)
Sudan
Ward Heneveld, (*U.S.A.*)
Kenya
Richard B. Heflebower, (*U.S.A.*)
Argentina
Bruce Herrick, (*U.S.A.*)
Venezuela
Susan Hickok, (*U.S.A.*)
Sahel
Sri Lanka
*Albert O. Hirschman, (*U.S.A.*)
Colombia
Warren P. Hogan, (*Australia*)
Pakistan
*William C. Hollinger, (*U.S.A.*)
Ghana
Pakistan
Robinson Hollister, (*U.S.A.*)
Ghana
Englehart Hondelink, (*Holland*)
Pakistan
Richard M. Hook, (*U.S.A.*)
Kenya
Edgar M. Hoover, (*U.S.A.*)
Liberia
Branko Horvat, (*Yugoslavia*)
Peru
Diane Hunt, (*U.K.*)
Kenya
William Hunt, (*U.S.A.*)
Nicaragua
*Samuel P. Huntington, (*U.S.A.*)
Malaysia
*W. Richard Huntington, (*U.S.A.*)
Sudan

Consultant, (*Nationality*)
HIID Overseas Assignment

Ramon Ilusorio, (*Philippines*)
ndonesia
*Henry D. Jacoby, (*U.S.A.*)
Argentina
Colombia
Johannis A. Jansen, (*Netherlands*)
Pakistan
*Glenn P. Jenkins, (*Canada*)
Indonesia
Sri Lanka
Barclay G. Jones, (*U.S.A.*)
Kenya
*Christine W. Jones, (*U.S.A.*)
Sahel
*Leroy Jones, (*U.S.A.*)
Indonesia
Alan G. Johnston, (*U.S.A.*)
Kenya
Friedrich Kahnert, (*Germany*)
Liberia
*John F. Kain, (*U.S.A.*)
Iran
John Kalmbach, (*U.S.A.*)
Indonesia
John Kaufman, (*U.S.A.*)
Iran
Roy B. Kelly, (*U.S.A.*)
Indonesia
Stewart W. Kemp, (*U.S.A.*)
Indonesia
*Nathan Keyfitz, (*U.S.A.*)
Indonesia
*Maurice D. Kilbridge, (*U.S.A.*)
Pakistan
Peter Kilby, (*U.S.A.*)
Malaysia
Richard King, (*U.S.A.*)
Argentina
Harvey J. Klemmer, (*U.S.A.*)
Liberia
Borje Kragh, (*Sweden*)
Argentina
Wilbert Krause, (*Canada*)
Indonesia

Consultant, (*Nationality*)
HIID Overseas Assignment

*David T. Kresge, (*U.S.A.*)
Colombia
Anne Krueger, (*U.S.A.*)
Indonesia
Korea
Debra Kruetzer, (*U.S.A.*)
Mali
Paul Kuznets, (*U.S.A.*)
Korea
*Simon S. Kuznets, (*U.S.A.*)
Argentina
Ethiopia
Korea
Malaysia
Armando Lago, (*U.S.A.*)
Nicaragua
Malcolm G. Lane, (*Australia*)
Indonesia
Howard S. Lapin, (*U.S.A.*)
Pakistan
Harvey Leibenstein, (*U.S.A.*)
Greece
*Wassily Leontief, (*U.S.A.*)
Pakistan
Guy LeMoine, (*France*)
Sahel
David K. Leonard, (*U.S.A.*)
Kenya
Dietrich Lerche, (*Germany*)
Indonesia
Donald R. Lessard, (*U.S.A.*)
Bolivia
Ecuador
David B. Lewis, (*U.S.A.*)
Kenya
*Jeffrey D. Lewis, (*U.S.A.*)
Bangladesh
Marc Lindenberg, (*U.S.A.*)
Venezuela
Sein Linn, (*U.S.A.*)
Indonesia
Wolfgang Linser, (*Austria*)
Indonesia
Richard Lockwood, (*U.S.A.*)
Venezuela

Consultant, (*Nationality*)
HIID Overseas Assignment

*Millard F. Long, (*U.S.A.*)
Ghana
Indonesia
Harold S. Luft, (*U.S.A.*)
Colombia
James A. Lynch, (*U.S.A.*)
Venezuela
Frank Lysy, (*U.S.A.*)
Malaysia
John D. MacArthur, (*U.K.*)
Ethiopia
Paul MacAvoy, (*U.S.A.*)
Indonesia
*Richard D. Mallon, (*U.S.A.*)
Colombia
Ecuador
Malaysia
Peru
Sri Lanka
Venezuela
Lawrence Mann, (*U.S.A.*)
Nicaragua
Robin Marris, (*U.K.*)
Venezuela
Brian V. Martin, (*U.K.*)
Pakistan
Kurt Martin, (*U.K.*)
Iran
Robert Martin, (*U.S.A.*)
Mali
*Edward S. Mason, (*U.S.A.*)
Ethiopia
Iran
Korea
Malaysia
Pakistan
*David H. P. Maybury–Lewis, (*U.K.*)
Ecuador
Indonesia
Sudan
Geoffrey W. Maynard, (*U.K.*)
Liberia

Consultant, (*Nationality*)
HIID Overseas Assignment

Alexander F. McCalla, (*Canada*)
Kenya
David S. McCauley, (*U.S.A.*)
Indonesia
Ross H. McLeod, (*Australia*)
Indonesia
Thomas McLeod, (*Canada*)
Iran
David E. McCloud, (*U.S.A.*)
Kenya
Charles E. McLure, (*U.S.A.*)
Indonesia
*Gerald McCue, (*U.S.A.*)
Iran
*Noel F. McGinn, (*U.S.A.*)
Indonesia
Korea
Malaysia
Charles E. McLure, Jr., (*U.S.A.*)
Malaysia
*Malcolm F. McPherson, (*Australia*)
Sahel
Micheline Mescher, (*U.S.A.*)
Indonesia
*John R. Meyer, (*U.S.A.*)
Colombia
Iran
Edwin Mills, (*U.S.A.*)
Korea
Richard Monteverde, (*U.S.A.*)
Indonesia
*John Montgomery, (*U.S.A.*)
Kenya
Theodore Moran, (*U.S.A.*)
Malaysia
David Morawetz, (*Australia*)
Bolivia
William Morsch, (*U.S.A.*)
Venezuela
Thomas H. Mugford, (*U.S.A.*)
Malaysia
Peggy B. Musgrave, (*U.S.A.*)
Indonesia
Nicaragua

Consultant, (*Nationality*)
HIID Overseas Assignment

*Richard A. Musgrave, (*U.S.A.*)
Indonesia
Korea
Philip Musgrove, (*U.S.A.*)
Venezuela
Charles Musselman, (*U.S.A.*)
Kenya
*Charles N. Myers, (*U.S.A.*)
Mali
Manning Nash, (*U.S.A.*)
Malaysia
James R. Nelson, (*U.S.A.*)
Colombia
Liberia
Dick Netzer, (*U.S.A.*)
Colombia
Maryam Niamir, (*Iran*)
Indonesia
Essama Nssah, (*Cameroon*)
Sahel
Marcia Odell, (*U.S.A.*)
Kenya
Oliver Oldman, (*U.S.A.*)
Colombia
Indonesia
Nancy Olewiler, (*U.S.A.*)
Indonesia
F. Bjorn Olsen, (*Denmark*)
Iran
Charles E. Olson, (*U.S.A.*)
Colombia
Roger G. Opie, (*U.K.*)
Pakistan
James Otto, (*U.S.A.*)
Kenya
Mead Over, (*U.S.A.*)
Sahel
Catherine A. Overholt, (*U.S.A.*)
Venezuela
James Paddock, (*U.S.A.*)
Ecuador
Richard B. Pagett, (*U.S.A.*)
Indonesia

Consultant, (*Nationality*)
HIID Overseas Assignment

John Palsrok, (*U.S.A.*)
Indonesia
*Gustav F. Papanek, (*U.S.A.*)
Ethiopia
Ghana
Greece
Indonesia
Liberia
Pakistan
Yung Chul Park, (*Korea*)
Sri Lanka
Stephen Parker, (*U.S.A.*)
Indonesia
Michael Parkin, (*U.K.*)
Indonesia
J. R. Parkinson, (*U.K.*)
Pakistan
Rodrigo Parot, (*Chile*)
Dominican Republic
Peter Parr, (*U.S.A.*)
Sudan
Richard H. Patten, (*U.S.A.*)
Indonesia
Pakistan
Mark R. Patterson, (*U.S.A.*)
Mali
Sudan
Arne A. Paulsen, (*U.S.A.*)
Greece
William J. A. Payne, (*U.K.*)
Sudan
Marc A. Pembroke, (*U.S.A.*)
Indonesia
George Perazich, (*U.S.A.*)
Venezuela
*Dwight H. Perkins, (*U.S.A.*)
China
Korea
Malaysia
Guillermo E. Perry, (*Colombia*)
Indonesia
The Gambia
*Ulrich Petersen, (*U.S.A.*)Bolivia
Indonesia

Consultant, (*Nationality*)
HIID Overseas Assignment

Thomas C. Pinckney III, (*U.S.A.*)
Kenya
Thomas Pinfold, (*Canada*)
Kenya
Satya Podar, (*Canada*)
Indonesia
Richard D. Pomp, (*U.S.A.*)
China
William Pounds, (*U.S.A.*)
Indonesia
Karl Price, (*U.S.A.*)
Indonesia
Catherine Prime, (*Australia*)
Indonesia
Susan Prysor–Jones, (*U.K.*)
Mali
Andrew C. Quale, Jr., (*U.S.A.*)
Indonesia
P. N. Rasmussen, (*Denmark*)
Iran
W. Brian Reddaway, (*U.K.*)
Ghana
D. Gene Reese, (*U.S.A.*)
Pakistan
*Robert Repetto, (*U.S.A.*)
Indonesia
Korea
John Richardson, (*U.S.A.*)
Indonesia
Charles Richter, (*U.S.A.*)
Colombia
Paul O. Roberts, (*U.S.A.*)
Colombia
Nicaragua
Barbara Robinson, (*U.S.A.*)
Korea
Marguerite S. Robinson, (*U.S.A.*)
Indonesia
Emery M. Roe, (*U.S.A.*)
Kenya

Consultant, (*Nationality*) HIID Overseas Assignment

*Michael Roemer, (*U.S.A.*)
Bangladesh
Bolivia
China
Indonesia
Kenya
Korea
Malaysia
Venezuela
*Peter P. Rogers, (*U.K.*)
Iran
Alvin Roseman, (*U.S.A.*)
Malaysia
H. David Rosenbloom, (*U.S.A.*)
Indonesia
Paul Rosenstein–Rodan, (*U.S.A.*)
Colombia
*Henry Rosovsky, (*U.S.A.*)
Ethiopia
Greece
Indonesia
Pakistan
Martin Rudd, (*U.K.*)
Pakistan
Saleck Ould Saleck, (*Mauritania*)
Sahel
Pascal Salin, (*France*)
Sahel
Sidney Saltzman, (*U.S.A.*)
Kenya
Celso Samaniego, (*Philippines*)
Indonesia
Nouhoum Sankare, (*Mali*)
Sahel
Susan Sawyer, (*U.S.A.*)
Venezuela
Gary Saxonhouse, (*U.S.A.*)
Korea
John T. Saywell, (*Canada*)
Kenya
Gerhard Schiefer, (*Germany*)
Kenya
Robert Schneider, (*U.S.A.*)
Sahel

Consultant, (*Nationality*) HIID Overseas Assignment

Wayne Schutjer, (*U.S.A.*)
Kenya
*Daniel Schydlowsky, (*Peru*)
Argentina
Colombia
Douglas A. Scott, (*U.S.A.*)
Ghana
*Hal S. Scott, (*U.S.A.*)
China
Indonesia
James Seale, (*U.S.A.*)
Sudan
*Marcelo Selowsky, (*Chile*)
Colombia
Sergio Sepulveda, (*U.S.A.*)
Venezuela
David Sharry, (*U.S.A.*)
Sudan
Edward S. Shaw, (*U.S.A.*)
Malaysia
Graham Keith Shaw, (*U.K.*)
Indonesia
John Sheahan, (*U.S.A.*)
Malaysia
Sri Lanka
Michael Shifter, (*U.S.A.*)
Venezuela
Carl S. Shoup, (*U.S.A.*)
Indonesia
Sahel
Donald S. Shoup, (*U.S.A.*)
Colombia
Liberia
Martin Shubik, (*U.S.A.*)
Colombia
Modibo Sidibe, (*Mali*)
Sahel
Katherine Sierra, (*U.S.A.*)
Indonesia
C. G. S. Simkin, (*New Zealand*)
Indonesia

Consultant, (*Nationality*)
HIID Overseas Assignment

*David N. Smith, (*U.S.A.*)
China
Indonesia
Liberia
Malaysia
Sri Lanka
*Arthur Smithies, (*U.S.A.*)
Argentina
Ethiopia
*Donald R. Snodgrass, (*U.S.A.*)
Indonesia
Korea
Malaysia
Budhy Soegijoko, (*Indonesia*)
Indonesia
Ralph Sorenson, (*U.S.A.*)
China
William F. Steel, (*U.S.A.*)
Ghana
*Joseph J. Stern, (*U.S.A.*)
Bangladesh
Malaysia
Pakistan
Sri Lanka
Richard Stibbs, (*U.K.*)
Iran
Cathy Strombom, (*U.S.A.*)
Iran
Cathy Douglas Stone, (*U.S.A.*)
Indonesia
James M. Stone, (*U.S.A.*)
Indonesia
Mahlon Straszheim, (*U.S.A.*)
Colombia
Alan Strout, (*U.S.A.*)
Indonesia
Nicaragua
Venezuela
J. Dirck Stryker, (*Mali*)
Sahel
*Lawrence H. Summers, (*U.S.A.*)
Indonesia
Emil Sunley, (*U.S.A.*)
Indonesia

Consultant, (*Nationality*)
HIID Overseas Assignment

*Stanley S. Surrey, (*U.S.A.*)
Indonesia
*Kenneth G. Swanberg, (*U.S.A.*)
Venezuela
*Lance Taylor, (*U.S.A.*)
Peru
Eric Teicholz, (*U.S.A.*)
Iran
Johanes Th. Thijsse, (*Netherlands*)
Pakistan
*John W. Thomas, (*U.S.A.*)
Ethiopia
Kenya
Liberia
Sudan
*C. Peter Timmer, (*U.S.A.*)
Indonesia
Kenya
Sri Lanka
Sadik Toksoz, (*Turkey*)
Sudan
Thomas P. Tomich, (*U.S.A.*)
Indonesia
Edward Tower, (*U.S.A.*)
Indonesia
Robert Travis, (*U.S.A.*)
Indonesia
Sandra Uhlig, (*U.S.A.*)
Indonesia
Miguel Urrutia, (*Colombia*)
Indonesia
Daniel Usher, (*Canada*)
Malaysia
Indonesia
David Vail, (*U.S.A.*)
Sudan
Peter van den Dool, (*U.S.A.*)
Indonesia
J. R. L. van den Elshout, (*Netherlands*)
Pakistan
Jan Hendrick van Leeuwen, (*Netherlands*)
Somalia
Willy van Rijckeghem, (*Belgium*)
Sahel

Consultant, (*Nationality*)
HIID Overseas Assignment

*Raymond Vernon, (*U.S.A.*)
Argentina
China
Colombia
Ghana
Indonesia
Liberia
John M. Villaume, (*U.S.A.*)
Sudan
Gregory Votano, (*U.S.A.*)
Iran
Otto G. Wadsted, (*Canada*)
Venezuela
Louis J. Walinsky, (*U.S.A.*)
Newfoundland
Brendan Walsh, (*Ireland*)
Iran
*Donald P. Warwick, (*U.S.A.*)
Indonesia
Malaysia
Richard S. Weckstein, (*U.S.A.*)
Liberia
Edward Weiler, (*U.S.A.*)
Sahel
Harold Wein, (*U.S.A.*)
Argentina
Linda Weiner, (*U.S.A.*)
Kenya
Myron Weiner, (*U.S.A.*)
Malaysia
Stanislaw H. Wellisz, (*U.S.A.*)
Liberia
Pakistan

Consultant, (*Nationality*)
HIID Overseas Assignment

*Louis T. Wells, Jr., (*U.S.A.*)
Ghana
Indonesia
Liberia
Malaysia
Sri Lanka
Clay G. Wescott, (*U.S.A.*)
Kenya
Marissa C. Weseley, (*U.S.A.*)
China
Indonesia
Robert L. West, (*U.S.A.*)
The Gambia
Fred M. Westfield, (*U.S.A.*)
Argentina
Frank Westhoff, (*U.S.A.*)
Indonesia
Charles Williams, (*U.S.A.*)
Indonesia
Edward L. Wheelwright, (*Australia*)
Argentina
Lawrence J. White, (*U.S.A.*)
Indonesia
George Wilson, (*U.S.A.*)
Malaysia
Lawrence H. Wortzel, (*U.S.A.*)
China
Stephen Hwa–Kuo Yeh, (*U.S.A.*)
Malaysia
*Marian Zeitlin, (*U.S.A.*)
Sudan

* Indicates persons who held Harvard corporation appointments at the rank of Instructor or above during or after their DAS/HIID service.